THE
WAYSHOWER

OTHER BOOKS BY JOHN-ROGER

Blessings of Light
Divine Essence
Dream Voyages
Forgiveness – The Key to The Kingdom
Fulfilling Your Spiritual Promise
God Is Your Partner
Inner Worlds of Meditation
Journey of a Soul
Living Love
Loving Each Day
Loving Each Day for Moms & Dads
Loving Each Day for Peacemakers
Manual on Using The Light
Passage Into Spirit
Psychic Protection
Relationships: Love, Marriage & Spirit
Sex, Spirit & You
Spiritual High (with Michael McBay)
Spiritual Warrior: The Art of Spiritual Living
The Consciousness of Soul
The Path to Mastership
The Power Within You
The Spiritual Family
The Spiritual Promise
The Tao of Spirit
Timeless Wisdoms, Vol. I
Timeless Wisdoms, Vol. II
Walking With the Lord
The Way Out Book
Wealth & Higher Consciousness
When Are You Coming Home? (with Pauli Sanderson)

OTHER BOOKS BY JOHN-ROGER with PAUL KAYE
Living the Spiritual Principles of Health and Well-Being
Momentum: Letting Love Lead
What's It Like Being You?
The Rest of Your Life
Serving & Giving
The Spiritual Principles of Abundance and Prosperity

THE
WAYSHOWER

JOHN-ROGER, DSS

MANDEVILLE PRESS
LOS ANGELES, CA

Mandeville Press
P.O. Box 513935
Los Angeles, CA 90051-1935
323-737-4055
jrbooks@mandevillepress.org
www.mandevillepress.org
www.msia.org

Printed in the United States of America
ISBN# 978-1-935492-76-4
Library of Congress# 2011906243

TABLE OF CONTENTS

INTRODUCTION

I MET JOHN-ROGER MANY YEARS AGO, AT A TIME WHEN I HAD NO AWARENESS THAT MY LIFE (OR ANYONE'S LIFE) HERE ON EARTH MIGHT REALLY BE A SPIRITUAL JOURNEY, A JOURNEY OF OUR SOULS.

But I loved to listen to the stories he told me of the experiences that had awakened him to something more, something deeper than what life appeared to be. I didn't necessarily understand all that he was telling me, but I was intrigued and inspired.

Oh, the stories he told me: of his lives in other times and other places (what he calls "far memory") where he won and lost the treasures of this world, rose and fell from power and prestige, put his faith in the illusions of this world, and then found out the hard way they were only illusions. They are stories of the wayshower ... and stories of the one being shown the way. Here, in this book, he shares some of his stories and his wisdom as the Wayshower.

When I first knew John-Roger, he often referred to "the boys upstairs." Because he lived in a top floor apartment at the time and there was no upstairs at all (so clearly there were no boys upstairs), I was mystified. In time and as he told me more stories of contact and communication with masters of Light beyond this physical realm, I came to understand "the boys upstairs" was code for those spiritual beings with whom he was working and from whom he was learning.

In the early days of our friendship, I sometimes found myself living within J-R's stories. We visited others who carried the gifts of far memory, who saw this world as a spiritual journey connected backwards and forward in time, who opened my eyes to the possibility of a reality that reached far beyond this physical reality. But it was in watching how J-R lived that I got my deepest lessons of Spirit. He saw the world through the lens of Spirit: What was the experience of the moment teaching him? How could he bring a spiritual perspective to all that was happening? How would "the boys upstairs" guide him? How well would he listen to the voice of loving and compassion that spoke from his true self?

I loved his humor and his perspective, his mix of reverence and irreverence. He could tell me the story of his encounter with an angel in the form of a hitchhiker and the next moment tell me about his favorite hamburger joint in Hollywood (and off we would go). One evening he might tell me of his spiritual journey in this life and how he came to accept the mantle of a spiritual consciousness he calls the Mystical Traveler or how his life's purpose was to bring awareness of soul transcendence to those who would also walk this spiritual path; and the next day, he might be helping me teach ballroom dancing to the kids at the school where we taught. Sometimes it seemed like we could ricochet from the spiritual balm of the "divine ocean of love and mercy" to body surfing at Manhattan Beach and the delights of frozen bananas.

John-Roger has been my wayshower since the moment we met. When I am struggling with the challenges of my life, he can help me see a greater reality in an instant. When I am unsure what choice to make in my physical life, he might say, "Remember, your job is soul transcendence," and I see that the physical level choice is not so critical; seeing my soul's Light within whatever choice I make is the point. When I'm disowning the parts of myself that aren't "measuring up," he might say, "Remember, you are someone to love," and I re-calibrate and come back to loving. And he has also shown me who I am in my soul, in my Spirit. It is a gift beyond measure.

Through the years I have had the good fortune to count myself as J-R's friend, student, and votary, I have come to know him as a true mystic (like someone from days of old when mystics were revered in our world as men of extraordinary wisdom, men who had achieved the direct experience of Spirit which surpassed the rest of us). I have learned that he began his quest to discover the deepest truth of God and man long, long ago—and it seems to me, in this lifetime, he is at the zenith of all he has learned through time. His stories of other lifetimes are fascinating. The wisdom with which he lives his life here and now is indisputable. The loving he consistently demonstrates for everyone and everything stands as one of his most magnificent achievements. It has been unbroken and unconditional for at least the 47 years I've known this Wayshower and speaks to me of God and Spirit in a way no words ever could. I cannot deny I want that kind of loving in my life, in my soul. So I go for it day after day after day and John-Roger is still showing me how to love better and deeper. He is still showing me how to recognize the illusions of separation and embrace the nature of the divine. He is still showing me how to laugh at myself and dance with God.

Here, in *The Wayshower*, John-Roger tells us some of his stories in his own words. He shares stories of his physical, emotional, and spiritual journeys ... in this and other lifetimes, how he came to learn how to be true to himself, to step beyond the fears his human consciousness thought were real, beyond the hurts experienced by his emotions and ego, and beyond his judgments and doubts. His stories show us how he discovered the reality that lies behind every illusion. And that reality is God. His stories light our way, if we realize that his story is also our story, not in the details but in the journey from darkness to Light, the journey from our false selves to our true selves, the journey of our Souls home to the heart of God. If you want to find the way to more joy, grace, and love in your life, read on or listen to his stories and see where they lead you.

Pauli Sanderson

THE WAYSHOWER

CHAPTER ONE

COMING INTO THE WORK I DO

I GUESS THAT I FIRST GOT STARTED IN DOING THIS WORK OUT OF CURIOSITY.

I figured there had to be more to life than what appeared to be so from this physical level, because if this were all there was, there did not seem to be much reason to be here. So that curiosity brought in a pretty intense type of inquiry that I applied to every aspect of my life. My questions became: who, how, what, where, why, when, how come, who did it, how much, and how often? And I studied, observed, watched, questioned, and experienced.

First I studied—at college, universities, seminaries, and so on. I became very adept with the intellectual information I read in books, but I soon discovered that if someone took away my books, there was nothing inside me that could sustain that "knowledge." Along with that discovery, I realized that different authors claimed different truths. When Einstein discovered the law of relativity, it wiped out many years of physics. I looked at that and realized that new materials were always refuting, transforming, and updating older materials. Nothing seemed to be permanent or certain. So a considerable amount of confusion set in, with an attitude of futility towards ever pinning down "knowledge." It seemed that if I followed what I read in books, I would always be following someone else's opinion, emotions, dogma, money, personality, or athletic prowess.

So I watched the ideals, expectations, and desires I had, and I found out that everyone had their own individual approach and that no one could ever successfully copy anyone else's approach. I saw that this just did not work. So I looked for what I could do. Within my consciousness I realized that if I could not go "first class," I would rather stay home, take it easy, and save my money. I decided I would just watch my own process of unfoldment and development and see where my own truth would lead me. I realized that I really did not care to be a world teacher or anything else like that. I just wanted to find out what was going on and to bear witness to the truth wherever I found it.

To begin with, I studied the Bible, and I also studied people's interpretations of the Bible. One group said, "Don't dance." Another group said, "It's okay to dance, but don't smoke or drink." And yet another group was going down to the basement for a cigarette and a beer while they discussed church business. I knew that what each group was saying was, "We're right and you're wrong," and that did not seem too possible. So I went back to the Bible to study some more.

I found out that the Bible said that the Word was made flesh and realized that the Word was not the building or the dogma or the ritual, but it was the people. So I started looking at all the people that I thought were truly uplifting. But I looked just at the flesh and realized that the flesh is often weak and that it fails. Then

I looked at the emotions, but I saw that they were too erratic to be the house of God. Then I looked at the mind and found confusion and contradiction. So that approach did not get me too far in my quest for God.

All along, there was growing within me a longing for Light and love and the manifestation of God in some form that I could identify and relate to. My prayer became "Lord, You can have the whole thing. I just want to know who You are." That prayer was being answered all along, though I was not yet recognizing it. I knew that I wanted a God that was in all things, that was present with everyone so that we could truly be a family of God and in God. I wanted a fellowship and a brotherhood, a oneness among all mankind. I could sense the reality of that in my heart, though I had, as yet, no objective reality to support that.

My friends soon decided that I "had religion," and I really hoped that that was so. I really hoped that what I felt within me to be so would not fall apart when it was tested. Sometimes my friends got tired of discussing my ideas, but I would sort of insist that they talk with me anyway. I was following my vision that said we could all arrive at a mutual understanding, a cooperation, an enthusiasm towards this life of God. I was positive that all that existed for us, and yet so much in the world seemed to tell me that this could not be so.

Our discussions seemed to be filled with disagreement and opposing points of view, but we came to one area that seemed to be a common meeting ground of experience. We knew that life, for each one of us, was involved with the process of breath. We thought maybe that was a process of the autonomic nervous system or the motor reflexes, but beyond that, I knew that breath was intimately connected to life and to Spirit and that everything that breathes has life in it. And life is awareness, which is Spirit, which is God.

My friends said, "That's nonsense."

I said, "Then I'll keep breathing in and out, and you stop," to which they all said no. So I said, "We have one thing in common. We all breathe in and out. Breath and the awareness of breath is the common denominator."

One time, swimming in a lake, I developed a cramp that was so severe that I had great difficulty staying on top of the water, much less swimming towards shore. I went down and came up, went down and came up, four or five times. On about the fifth trip up for air, I realized that I really might drown, and the intensity of that realization and the desire for life and for that next breath moved my consciousness in a way it had never been moved before. I broke the cramp and found that I moved through the water so dynamically that it was almost as if the shore reached out and pulled me up. I recognized the tremendous force of life that was within me and the tremendous desire to continue with that life. It was a lesson in the awareness of breath that certainly locked into my consciousness the sacredness of life.

There were several incidents in my life when I walked very close to physical death. There were illnesses, accidents, and all sorts of strange situations. The catastrophes always seemed to disperse before anything happened that was too damaging. But through it all, I kept breathing in and breathing out. I knew what I was doing and that my prime directive through those times was to keep breathing.

In the midst of the turmoil and the confusion that always seemed to be present around me, I said, "If I could just get away from this physical body for a little while and look at things clearly, maybe I could see what is going on. Maybe I could get free of the delusions and the ego and all the games I must be playing on myself. Maybe that's the approach: to 'see yourself as others see you.'" But I did not know how to do that, so I continued along in the confusions of the moment and gradually began to realize that other people saw me through their own set of illusions, delusions, and ego approaches. I then realized that to see myself as others saw me probably would not help me a great deal.

It was getting to be the time in life when I should have chosen a career. So I started looking around at what I would like to do, and I decided that I would like to be a professional person. After all, everybody who was anybody was a professional person. It was popular. I thought that I should have a degree, so I got a university degree in psychology. I thought that was pretty good, and so did my family and friends. Then I went out to look for a job.

I applied for one job, and they asked me if I had a degree. I said yes, and they said, "You're too qualified for this job." So I applied for another job, and they said, "You need a master's degree for this job." I was too good for one, not good enough for another, and so it went. I found out that that piece of paper I had worked so hard for was not worth all that much. Finally on one job interview, I was asked if I had a degree, and I said no. I was hired on the spot. It was not long before I found a job that I liked better, so I quit. People told me, "It's not good to jump jobs so quickly."

I said, "Come on, don't lay out more 'scripture' on me and tell me how it 'should' be. I don't want this job, so I'm leaving. I don't want to come back to it or I wouldn't go. I'm not afraid to quit. I'm going on to a better job, and from there, I'll go to an even better job." In this, I discovered a little bit more of my truth and realized that sometimes there can be awakening and realization through personal rejection and maybe even a little hostility. I also began to know that life must be lived according to the truth of the moment.

I began to notice, too, that my bumbling ways, my mistakes and doing things wrong, somehow always turned out right. That was interesting. It got to the point where I would tell a lie—a blatant, audacious, out-and-out lie—and it would turn out to be true. One week I said, "I'm going to get a new car." I could not even afford the one I was driving, but in about a week, it just happened that I got a great deal and was soon driving a new car. I had even forgotten my lie until a friend said, "Hey, you did get a new car," and I realized that another "lie" had come true. So I started looking at the knower inside that is aware of things long before the consciousness knows what is happening.

THE WAYSHOWER
CHAPTER TWO

THE TRUE SELF

SOME OF THE GREATEST PEOPLE IN THE WORLD HAVE SAID SOMETHING LIKE, "KNOW THYSELF" AND "TO THINE OWN SELF BE TRUE."

When I was around twenty, I saw this across the top of a high school in San Francisco: "To thine own self be true." I remember stopping the car and thinking, "Why would they want to put something so confusing on the top of a high school? Why don't they put something like 'Health, wealth, and happiness'?" That's universal; everybody wants to be healthy, wealthy, and happy. But "to thine own self be true" seemed to me such a waste of time.

Shortly after that, I had an opportunity to talk to the president of my college and asked him, "What do you think about this: 'To thine own self be true'?"

He said, "That's a very beautiful statement, a very marvelous statement."

I told him, "I was quite taken up with this, also. One thing I didn't quite understand, and maybe you can clarify it for me because you're a man of letters, why did he say something like that?"

As I recall, the answer was something like "Well, to know yourself is to know all things."

"That's fine," I said. "How do you know when you know yourself?"

He said, "I thought you were going to ask something like that." The president of the college was negligent in his ability to know who this self is.

So I decided that if this great philosopher could say something like "to thine own self be true," then this mediocre boy could understand what it means, because he didn't say it in a complex way.

So I started thinking about the idea and placed myself in a quest to locate this. Soon after that, I was browsing through the library stacks at the university, and I felt this funny feeling come over me. I thought I might get a little dizzy, that maybe the room should have a little more air in it, a little more oxygen, that it was a little stuffy. I tried to identify the feeling many, many ways, but since I couldn't identify it, I figured, "Well, I'm here, so I'll just put up with it."

I sort of flowed with this feeling, and it wasn't too long until I had a book out of the shelf called *Moby Dick*. I read where it said, "Roll on, thou deep and dark blue ocean, roll!" and I thought, "That's rather a profound statement, because that's what it's going to do anyway." That was like pointing at a light and saying, "The light's on," and pointing at the roof and saying, "That's the roof." It's obvious knowledge, so why bother my head with that? That shows you where I was: I was intellectually "tripping." But I wasn't even aware of what was being shown to me, and I was still too smart to see.

Thumbing through the book some more, I came across a part where Captain Ahab was speaking. He said something like, "Who is moving this hand? Is it I, Captain Ahab? Is it God? Is it something else that moves this hand? Who does it?" I thought, "That is the question I have been asking: *who's doing it?*"—because it seemed to me that when you're not doing it, you're doing it anyway. When you're not thinking of walking, you're walking anyway. When you're not thinking of driving your car, you're doing it anyway. Who is doing it?

I decided maybe the psychologists had the answer, so I approached various ones and asked, "Who does this?"

Some said, "Oh, that's just the unconscious." I asked where it was, and they said, "It's below the level of consciousness." So I asked where *that* was, and they said, "Well, we haven't located it."

I said, "Then how do you know that's what's doing it?" Of course, the answer to that is very beautiful: because it's not being done consciously; it's being done unconsciously. So they won, but at the same time they lost, because I had to dismiss them since they were unable to solve the question of who this self is.

I also had an opportunity to speak to a psychiatrist and asked, "Who is this?"

He said, "That's the old, ancient part of the brain, the cerebellum. It's located in the back of the head, down by the spinal cord."

I asked its function, and he said, "We don't know all of its function."

I asked, "Does it drive the car for me?"

He said, "Well, no, I don't think so. It's more on the animal level of responses."

"Like anger and temper?"

He said, "Yeah, probably more along that line."

So I asked him, "Do anger and temper drive cars?"

He asked me, "What's that got to do with it?" So I explained to him what the one psychologist had said to me. The psychiatrist said, "Well, he's wrong. Those psychologists don't know what they're talking about."

I said, "Maybe I should go to one more psychologist," and he said, "No, save yourself the search."

So I told him, "I would like to know who the self is and what 'to thine own self be true' means."

He started to say, "Well, now, according to Freud, ..." and I said, "I would like to know according to *you*. I could go read Freud's books, too. I'm here to save time; I'm here out of expediency. I've got to get to this self, whatever it is."

He asked me, "Why is it driving you?" and I said, "Because this is something that everybody says you have to be true to. And I'd like to at least know what it is."

He then said, "Why don't you go to a minister?" and I realized that he was very gracefully bowing out. I wasn't sure if it was because of incompetence, ineptness, or not knowing, but, at any rate, I just said okay.

So I went to quite a few ministers and asked them all, "Who is this self in 'to thine own self be true'?" One asked how to spell it, and I said, "I don't know if it's a capital *s* or a small *s*." He said that it makes a difference, so I said, "You decide and tell me both."

He said, "The Self with a capital *s* would be the higher consciousness, and the self with the small *s* is the lower consciousness."

I said, "You've got yourself in the same corner that everybody else has. You've played with words. Is there a key, is there a mechanism, is there a method, is there a hocus-pocus, an abracadabra, is there something where I can identify within me so I can know?"

He told me, "I don't think you can ever know because your mind is too inquisitive."

"Well, okay," I said. "Then that means you and I have shut off communication."

"Apparently."

I said, "I'm sorry. It wasn't shut off on my end," and he said, "Well, I think I shut it off on my end."

"Is it because you don't know?"

He said, "I don't know," and I said, "That makes two of us."

He told me, "If you find out, will you let me know?" and I said, "I just pray to God that I find out because it seems to be important."

He said, "Maybe you should identify who the self is," and right then and there, this fellow who had shut off communication gave me encouragement. If I'm going to be true to something, maybe I should identify what it is, what this self is.

So I looked in many, many religious books for all the religious reference points that I could find. This is the synopsis of all they said: God is good. God is everywhere. God is in all things, manifesting differently according to the mechanism that God is functioning through.

I also talked to a lot of educators, and it finally came out that if I were going to find out who the self was, I'd better do it myself. The religious questing hadn't done it for me. In many ways, I really wished it would have, but then, if it had, we would not have ventured into these whole new ideas of spiritual unfoldment: if it's good, it will work for you, and if it's not working for you, get to what works for you. Build your life upon your knowledge. Let your belief lead you forward and your faith tell you it's going to be there. But don't live in your tomorrows when you have to live right now. And make these right nows work.

At that time, I was very frantic, like, "By God, let's work this." So I went out to a place called Land's End in San Francisco. It was one of those nights when the fog comes rolling up and the Coast Guard station is sending out its sound. It was a very mystical evening, and I thought, "This is a perfect evening for vampires and monsters and werewolves." Then I thought, "Now, why did I do that? Why did I go that way when there's nothing there?" Something inside me said, "What a beautiful, interesting, mystical, spiritual night." It was like a baptism of the mist—with vampires and goblins and everything hiding behind the trees. And I kept thinking, "Why did *that* come in here? Who is doing that? And who is doing the 'beautiful, wonderful' thing?"

I saw that I had two points of view, and I did neither one of them, as far as I knew. So I asked, "Which one is the culprit?" Something deep inside me said, "Why waste your time trying to solve something like this? Don't be stupid. There are a lot of things you can do. Why don't you go dancing?"

A bar called the Red Robin was down the street from me, and it had beautiful go-go girls that weren't quite go-go yet. I figured that would be pretty good because it was going to be chilly outside before too long. So I got in my car and zipped down to what's known as the Tenderloin. My parking place was right out in front, so I knew it was right. It was very interesting in there. The music was very loud, which was very good. The girls were very much undressed, which was also very good, and what wasn't undressed was very okay because I had a very good imagination.

I was enjoying myself there for about two hours until all of a sudden I got this tremendous strain, like, "What are you doing here? Don't you know you're just wasting your time here? You're not being true to yourself." And almost faster than you could say, "Split," I was out of that bar, standing out in the street and saying, "Now who on earth did that? I was very happy and contented in all of that."

So I went to my car and figured, "The whole weekend, the whole evening, is absolutely ruined. And what am I doing in a cold town like this, anyway? I wasn't born here, I'm just here going to school. So I'll study and get the schooling done and get out of here."

I got home and started on the books and something said, "You're not going to finish the schooling tonight anyway, but there is this great little Italian restaurant up on Knob Hill that has some very nice food. Some nice people go in there. Why don't you go up and see what's going on?" So I was in the car going up to see what was going on. I loved it. I spent three or four hours there, and when I got through there, it was close to four or five in the morning. I decided I had better leave because I had to get some rest before I had to go to work, before I had to leave work and go to school, before I had to do other things.

That was one of those miserable days where you're sleepy and you almost come close to wrecking the car a few times. Then you cuss out the guy on the street, and you're just hoping that he'll stop and maybe give you the "American greeting" so you can get out and poke him right in the nose. I'm not a fighter, so while all this was going on, I thought, "How ridiculous. If he went to hit me, I'd jump. I'd talk the guy out of it and make him look like a fool." But part of me just wished he'd try it.

So that was a miserable day. I went to school for the things that I really had to have and was there to learn, but all I felt like doing was sleeping. It was like, "Oh, Lord, would you just shut up and open some windows and get some coffee in here?" Then I had to run home and go to bed to sleep a few hours before I did some other things. But I slept all night long and missed one of the nicest parties in the history of San Francisco. When I heard about it the next morning, I was so depressed and miserable that I was moaning because there were people there I really wanted to meet.

I was telling some friends about all these things that were going on, and one of them said, "You're stupid!"

I said, "Well, yes, but it's not my fault. I'm a very intelligent person. And look, I'm out here by myself in this big city. I'm doing very well for myself, and I know a lot of nice people. I have a nice car, when I can afford to drive it." I absolutely disregarded what that person said because they didn't know what they were talking about. I looked at them and wondered, "Who are you?" They were actually my teacher, but I missed it.

So I decided that what I needed was a little spiritual consoling. There was a Methodist church on the corner, which always seemed to be open then. I'd go there and sit and look at that cross. It was a beautiful thing with the lights on it. You'd get that funny feeling sitting there, and suddenly a few tears would come. You'd look around to see if there was anybody watching because, after all, if there were, there'd be something in your eye, and if there weren't, then you'd just let it out.

I'd sit there thinking, "Here I am in some form of a religious communication, and, by God, I'm afraid somebody's going to see me if I cry. Then why don't I just get out of here and go someplace else?" So I did. When I got outside,

I said to myself, "Who told you to get out of there?" I thought I was splitting myself apart, probably going crazy. It was very interesting.

So I decided that this time I would go back in the church and sit there until I got an answer. I was sitting in there, and I got the answer: God is good, and He's in everything, and He's everywhere. When He got through creating the earth, He looked at it and said, "It's good."

Then I asked myself, "Why do I have depression and doubt? And why, when I know I've got to study, do I take off and do other things? And why, when I know the car's low on gas and I don't fill it up, do I keep driving and thinking that maybe a miracle's going to happen? And I know if I park that car there, they're going to give me a ticket."

I was actually pretty famous in San Francisco for a little while. I parked anywhere and everywhere, except in front of fire hydrants—because they'd tow your car away. But anyplace else, they'd just give you a ticket. In two years, I had enough tickets to paper one side of my wall. My thinking was, "Who's going to pay them? I mean, they'd never catch me. After all, they're a bunch of dummies."

The day they did catch up with me was very funny. I saw these two guys coming towards me, and I knew: policemen. So I just looked at them and started laughing. There was already a ticket on the car, and I had wrapped it around my finger and was going to roll it up in a little ball and put it in my pocket.

One of the policemen came towards me, and I said, "Are you after this?"

He said, "Are you the owner of that?"

I said, "No, I think it's got your name on it."

He took it and said, "Yes, that's my name, but it's really meant for you. And I'd like you to put your name on it and on the original, too."

So I did, and I promised that I'd appear in court, which is a whole different world. Crime doesn't pay, and I learned right then that dishonesty forfeits divine aid. But I never knew where I was being dishonest. I knew I couldn't drive the car when it was out of gas, and then I'd get a ticket because I couldn't move my car. Then I thought, "What difference does it make? They're going to give me a ticket anyway, so I'll just park it even if I'm not out of gas. So go ahead and ticket it." It was the same thing in my mind, but, still, something would always say, "Who are you kidding?"

I knew that after two years I was going to leave the city and state, and they didn't know where I was going, so those tickets would all be gratis on the city. Well, they gave me a good deal. I think I parked anywhere I wanted to in San Francisco for about two and a half years for fifty cents a day.

I remember the judge, a beautiful man. He looked at me and said, "What do you think you're doing?" and I said, "I think I was getting away with it."

He sat there and asked me questions, and I just answered him, but my attitude wasn't too good. It was like, "What can he do with me, kill me?" And inside me, it was, "Don't try. Don't do that!"

The judge said, "Do you feel sorry about where you've been parking?"

I said, "No, I don't feel sorry for where I've been parking. But I'm not going to do it anymore."

"Well," he said, "that was my next question. Did you learn?"

I said, "Oh, sure. It isn't fun to stand here in front of you and this prosecuting attorney."

He asked me what I was doing down here, and I just looked him in the eye and laid the whole thing out to him. He said, "What are you looking for?"

I said, "I'm looking for myself."

He asked, "Have you seen a psychiatrist?"

When I said yes, he asked, "What did he say to you?"

"He said he couldn't find it either."

The judge told me to go to a minister, and I told him I'd been to several. I told him the names of all the people I had seen—the professors, the psychologists, the psychiatrist, the ministers. He asked, "Aren't you ashamed of it?"

I said, "I wasn't there for help, as if I were sick. I was searching. I'm looking for my own self—the self in 'to thine own self be true.'"

He just said, "Good luck!" And it hit me. He didn't say, "Good luck." He said "God luck."

Something inside me started saying, "Hey, dumdum, listen." And I also thought, "I'm not going to listen to all that stuff." I was starting to find out who the self was, and every time I'd get a little insight into it, it would scare me. I'd think, "You mean, that's in me? Oh, come on! That's more than I want to look at. I don't think I ... oh, no!"

But every once in a while, I'd see past that and see something very beautiful and very glorious, and I'd say to myself, "You know, I think you've been working hard. You should go down to the Red Robin and watch the girls dance tonight." And I also thought, "There has to be something here that is pushing me. Is it just the male urges? ... Yeah, probably that's got a lot to do with it. But it urges me to do an awful lot of things. And how come I can't control myself when I'm being pushed around by urges? And if I don't do it, I get depressed. And if you don't do it the way I want you to do it, I get depressed. And if you do it the way I want you to do it, I'm still depressed because then I can't respect you because you're weak, and I don't want to be around weak people. I want to be around strong people." I thought I was pretty weak, and if I were around strong people, then I would feel strong and then worthwhile, really good inside ... but for how long?

Eventually, I found out that there are two selves: one is the true self, and one is the false self. When that hit me, it really rocked me because here I was, waking up in the morning, battling inside myself, and taking it out on the world. If I got up in the morning and started looking through the false self, then it was, "Oh, no, morning, and I wonder if I can sleep another hour," because I was up on the wrong side of my head. I was certainly up on the wrong side of my self.

It went into my job doing investigation work. The boss would say, "You missed a point on investigation," and I'd say, "Why don't you go out there and do it yourself?"

He said, "Don't get angry at me. I'm saying this to help you," but my point of view was, "Who needs your help?"

He said, "You do. You missed the point."

I didn't want to hear that. Something inside me said, "You're the boss because you can't do anything else. And you're going to be the boss when I'm the *owner* of this place, but you're going to be boss under *me*." That told me that I had a false self going that was getting all out of proportion to what was going on.

Finally one day, I ate some humble pie. I think it was the day I really got into my true self. I went up to my boss and said, "I quit."

He was very surprised and said, "You're going to walk out the door?"

"No," I told him, "I'll do it your way."

He said, "That's the *first* thing you've done my way."

I said, "Well, don't push it." I was getting back in the false self again, and I thought, "I'll hit you in the nose." If I had, he'd have killed me, and you know how bad it hurts when somebody's going to kill you. If they do it, it's easy, but it's the *fear* that they're going to and not knowing when or how—and all that is part of a false self.

I had found out that I had my false self so wrapped up with the true self that I was having the devil of a time separating them. But it was actually pretty easy because all I had to do was find out, 'What is the state of God?' I asked a lot of people because I didn't know, and some said, "God is good and happiness and joy."

I asked, "How come there's so much misery and pestilence and death and despair on the planet?"

They'd look at me and say, "That's man's doing."

"Really? God is everywhere and is all things and in man. Then why is man doing it?"

"Well," they said, "you're very knowledgeable. *You* find out."

I had quested myself right out of their assistance. And when you're walking the path of spiritual righteousness—and I really felt I was right—you're usually in this path of spiritual wrongness. It takes great courage to say, "You know, I didn't know that," and when you do say that, you're residing in the true self. Or if somebody tells you something and you look at them and *don't* say, "Stupid" in your mind or out loud, you're residing in the true self.

I found out that inside me, the true self was very strong, so strong that it didn't worry how far the false self went. It didn't even care. I thought, "What a schnook. I mean, it's so strong it knows that anytime it wants to, it can instantly overtake the false self." Then I wondered how it would do this, and the more I thought about it, the funnier it got. I found myself just laughing, having myself a great time, and right there was one of the answers: it overcomes it through humor. That was one of the biggest keys. Then joy came in on top of it, and all of a sudden, I started getting this buoyancy inside me, and I thought that my insides were going to burst and that I'd be all over the whole town with this joy. It got so much, I had to back off. I had to go out and get depressed.

The false self is so easily recognized because it's the one that puts up the front. It says, "Look at me: lovely, charming, witty, wealthy, man-about-town, virile, and I can swear, too"—all the things that are fantastic. It says, "I've been here and I've been there," even if you haven't, because who's going to check? Then along comes somebody who says, "Where did you say you were?" You tell them, and they say, "Oh, the green house on the corner?"—and they've pierced the veil.

You say, "Get away! Who do you think you are, pushing on me?" Then they get you cornered, and you say, "Oh, it was a different town. Yeah, that's right, it was a different town."

About this time, you see that you have destroyed yourself in the eyes of everyone around you. But the thing of it is, all they have to say is, "Gee, you're neat," and up comes the false self again.

I also realized that the false self had the ego tucked in it so neatly, and it had vanity and pride in there, too. But I knew these were things I just didn't have; I knew it because I'd never seen it. My friends had told me I was a little conceited, but I knew that wasn't so, because to be conceited would be to have a fault, and I knew I didn't have any.

So I went to a very dear friend I studied with. He was like the president's son, and that was my "in" to get my diploma in case I didn't do something required. That was also the false self playing the game.

He told me, "You know, you're a very dear friend of mine."

I said, "That's true." And I was thinking, "And you're lucky!"

He went on, "But one of these days, you're going to open your eyes and see that you're a horse's ass."

I said, "That's true, too," because, for a moment there, something said, "Look and listen because this guy's going to read your beads." I was getting sick inside—my stomach was turning over—and I felt like the Tower of Babel with all my false images going down. I couldn't even talk clearly.

He sat there and proceeded to point out every false thing I had going. This idiot, this numskull, this nothing, this nobody nailed me down in about twenty-two minutes. And then he spent three hours giving me hankies as I cried myself silly.

There are all sorts of techniques that the false ego uses, and one is to say something like, "Yeah, you're right, I'm really no good." That is their cue to say, "Oh, no, you really *are* good," and then you say, "How?" and you're right back in it again.

But he was very smart. I said, "I'm no good," and he said, "I'm glad you can see it."

I was afraid to say, "Which part are you referring to?" because I knew he'd tell me. But I had this inquisitive mind, so I asked, and he told me. God bless him. He was right in every way. I thought, "You must be the savior back on the planet, because it's like you've been walking right with me all along."

We got all through, and he said, "Any comments?"

I said, "No, I think I'm going to have to go think about this," and he said, "Okay."

I ran home, packed my clothes, got in my car, and left the state. It was more than I could take—I thought.

So I went to another school and did some more schooling. One day I was sitting on top of a big, high mountain. (For some reason, I get up on big, high mountains and climb up big, tall trees because it takes a lot more to run away when you're captured someplace.) It happened to be up in Salt Lake City over the place where Brigham Young said, "This is the place." I used to say, "This is the place, drive on to California," because I didn't care for that state. But it was so funny, because no matter what state I was in, I didn't care for it. I didn't even care for my own state. Inside myself, it was a state of confusion and anxiety. It was often a state of despair and depression. I was the one who was producing it. I was producer, director, and actor, but nobody was buying tickets, and I was going broke.

It's a terrible feeling to find out you're going broke on yourself. It's one thing to be broke physically and not have a dollar in your pocket. It's another thing to be broke emotionally where you just don't want to be hurt anymore. And it's another thing to be broke mentally where you just can't take another idea because your mind is full. But to be bankrupt spiritually is absolute death, and I was on the brink of spiritual bankruptcy.

But I didn't even know it because I still had good old false self, who, I knew, was going to take me right to the grave. I also knew that when I went into the grave, it would separate and wait for me in another incarnation. Then, when I came back in, it was going to be right there, and we were going to play this game of musical lives again. But something inside me said, "You're not going to play it any longer."

It was that point where, like falling down on my hands and knees, I said, "Okay, Lord, for God's sake, my sake, help—whatever, whatever." I didn't get hit with a bolt of lightning or anything else, but I was hoping. If He'd have just done that at the time— thunder, a little breeze, something. The flies didn't even bother me. If I'd been bitten, I'd at least have said, "Ah, a sign, an omen!" It didn't come in like that.

I went on and got my education, finished up some degrees, and decided I'd go to Arizona. I was a pretty sharp counselor at the time and really knew some techniques. I could reach right into where people lived and grab hold of the chink in their armor and shake it up and down. Just give me thirty seconds with somebody, and I could absolutely destroy them. I knew the words, I knew how to say it, I knew how to look at them because I'd been trained by the experts, who taught me how you can manipulate words. I used to think to myself, "Why did I learn that? I can put you down in thirty seconds, and while you're trying to get up, I can kick you in the teeth, and I can take care of you for all next week, too, if I want to." I realized there was a lot of power in all of that, and I also realized that it was a negative thing.

Arizona didn't pan out, and I ended up in Southern California and looked around to see who was going to be the savior. The Bible said he's going to be back, and everybody was saying he's already here someplace, so I figured, "I'll know it." I mean, why wouldn't I know it? After all, look who I was.

So I went on what would be called a spiritual quest. For about three years, I devoted every second I could to it. Whenever that false self came in, where I'd look at somebody and judge, I'd go up to that person and say, "I'm sorry. I apologize." They'd look at me like, "You weird person."

I figured, "That's your ego trip. Someday you're going to be going through what I'm going through, but I'm getting out of it."

Another thing that kept coming back in was that I'd think, "I'm going to go do this," and somebody would say, "You don't have to do that. That's not going to make any difference. It's not going to work anyway."

That was when doubt became a very good friend of mine. Every time it came in on something, I knew that was the thing I should do. It seemed to want to block me. I had given so much energy into the negative self that it had full authority over my life, and it was doing a good job. When I'd close those doors at night and was by myself, lying on that bed, the walls and ceiling would seem to come in, and I'd sometimes think, "Oh, my God. There's got to be more than this." I wanted to get to sleep, but I'd be tense, tossing and turning all night long, thinking, "When am I going to go to sleep?"

I finally decided that the only thing I had to do was to find the true self. And when I found that, all other things would be in proper perspective.

Doing that didn't take too long, and it took a series of tremendous emotional illnesses that disturbed me. They didn't make me go crazy, but they made me look very carefully about where I was putting my next foot. They made me very careful about what I was going to put in motion. I was wrapping up karma in a hurry, but nobody was there to tell me.

The body was also going through all sorts of physical disturbances, so I went to a doctor, who said, "You're a very sick person. Your body's falling apart."

I said, "Yeah, I know. You ought to get in here with me if you can stand the pain."

The doctor told me I needed surgery, and I agreed. We talked sometime in November, and I suggested the following year, but he said I had to have it before the first of the year. So I told my friends, "Well, I'm dying. This is it."

So my mother came on the scene. You know, mothers are extremely valuable. They come on the scene, and if we don't watch it, they'll let us build our false ego. I told her, "I hate to say this, but I want to let you know I've made out a will, and you're getting all this."

She said, "Oh, my son! Don't do that. You're my ..." and I started feeling a little sorry for myself. But then I thought, "Am I going to go back into this? I'm through with it." There I was, getting the law of reversibility explained to me—how things are going to cycle back on us—but, again, nobody was there to tell me about it.

I would sit in the corner and get all wrapped up in that and wonder, "What is this?" And I realized, "I've got to get away from the body in order to see what this is. I can't see it while I'm here because it's got me buffaloed. If somebody goes, 'Boo,' I jump and run."

Then came the big day when they performed surgery on me. Before they put me out, I said, "Hey, I want you all to know that everything's just beautiful and fine," and away I went into the netherworld of not knowing what was going on. I woke very rapidly in high consciousness. There were all these people standing around, and I said, "Well, I died." It was pretty nice, but everything was a little hazy, and I couldn't see too clearly. They explained to me what was going on and let me look at some things and life patterns, and they said, "Now, you're going to go back in the body, and you're going to do these things."

So I said, "Yes, I will. I'm going to go back in and I'm going to do it."

You know, when we're on the other side, we're so sure of everything. We see it in pure spiritual knowledge, and we know that it's all right and proper and good and fantastic. So, naturally, we blow it and come back here, and that's when we think, "How come I'm here?" The answer is because we chose it. We may think, "Oh, no. I wouldn't have chosen this," and this is the false self doing the destructive work. The true self sees it in all our spiritual fulfillment.

So I managed to come back into the physical body. I rolled over in the bed and looked at this woman who was sitting there. She said, "Are you all right?"

I said, "Sure," and she immediately called for a nurse and said, "He's not all right."

I said, "Yeah, I'm all right," and then it was like, "Where am I? What's going on?" This is because I had a different consciousness with me, and things had sort of shifted. I looked at this woman, and she said, "Do you know who I am?"

I said, "Yeah, I think I know who you are."

She said, "I'm your mother."

And I said, "No, you're not. You gave birth to the physical body, but I think you should know right now that you're not my mother." Then she knew something was wrong. I told her, "I don't need a mother, but would you mind being an older friend? I think I really need an older friend tremendously." And she decided that she would be my older friend—until she could be my mother.

That was a shifting of consciousness, which happened in 1963, where I was allowed to walk around and experience this consciousness through a physical body. In a way, I guess I could call myself one of the fortunate ones, because once you find the true self, you have found your Christ light within, you've found your own God center. You have found that all things are right and proper, and one immeasurable thing you find is a serenity within you that urges you upward. It won't urge you to go to the local go-go bar or run to the local pastrami joint at three in the morning. It just urges you upward into a higher consciousness. It always says, "I can," and rarely ever says, "I'll try." It just says, "I'll do that," or "I'll look into it."

These two selves are inside us, and we do not reinforce our negative self. If we do, we get ourselves in a constant state of trouble. Our negative self pulls energy from negativity, from the physical-earth surroundings, from our out-of-balance situations. It exists here on the physical plane with us and is one of the most fantastic sentries. For example, it will give you nightmares if you don't do enough in the daytime.

The true self does not really reside here; it resides in Spirit. Spirit is everywhere, but I mean that the true self doesn't reside here in the physical. We find it by going back into our spiritual self. And when you have been in that consciousness, you'll look at this world and say, "It's so beautiful. Everything is right and proper."

THE WAYSHOWER

CHAPTER THREE

SEARCH FOR
A MASTER

THERE IS A GOOD QUESTION THAT EVERYBODY SEEMS TO BE ASKING INSIDE:

"Why am I having such a difficult time making the Soul (which is my true self, my true being, my contact with God) function and work here in this world—so that I can more consciously have joy and have it more abundantly, so that I am able to choose the valuable things in life that I want, so that I don't have to go through heartache and sorrow and suffering, etc.?"

God knows I asked that question many, many times. And one day I decided that if I could *ask* a question, there certainly had to be an answer—somewhere, somehow, someplace—that could soothe the mind and the emotions so that my body would feel good. Then it dawned upon me that if it's *my* body, then somebody else is speaking, not the body. And if I was saying *my* mind and *my* emotions, then I knew that I wasn't the emotions or the mind. So who was doing the talking? Who was the one complaining?

So I asked myself, "Who's complaining?" and the answer was, "The one who's unsatisfied is complaining, because everybody's not doing everything the way you want them to, the way you think it should be done." Of course, I thought that it was only reasonable that they do it my way, the way it "should" be done.

I would ask people how they saw things. I'd lay out a hypothetical, third-person situation that was actually real because it was about me all the time. I'd lay it out in detail and give my conclusion. Then it was like, "Don't you agree?" They'd agree, but really they didn't. I was programming their responses so I could feel better about my mistakes.

(The reason I knew they were mistakes is because they kept hurting. I had said, "This hurts, so this is a mistake." Saying that was actually my biggest mistake—because it might not be a mistake even though it hurt. It might just be an error in perception, an error in consciousness.)

I would justify why I did something so I could feel good even though others were feeling bad. I'm sure this is rather typical of man's progression across the planet: "I want this at any expense, even if it's at your expense." And I was getting answers very favorable to my point of view because I was asking my friends, who would give me points of view advantageous to me. But I wasn't solving anything with what my friends were telling me.

One day, out of desperation, I wondered who really were my friends, because I saw that they were telling me what I wanted to hear but what I also knew was not working. So I asked somebody who had made a point to tell me they didn't like me. I laid out the situation as a third-person story, and the person told me exactly how they saw it, which was precisely opposite of what everybody else had been telling me. I was very hurt to hear the truth because I had relegated truth to my own way of thinking and being—and that was it. I figured, "Because that person dislikes me, they are prejudiced, and they really knew I was talking about myself."

So I went to many people who were neither friends nor enemies but who were disinterested; they were neutral and didn't care if they saw me again. They started telling me much the same thing that my "enemy" was telling me, but in a way where I could also work with the information. I must have talked to somewhere around fifty to sixty people about this particular thing that, to me, was a tremendous problem. If anybody had found out, I would have felt absolutely ruined.

This problem was my not sitting down and doing my studies when I knew I should. The more I talked to people, the more I started finding out that the cure was to sit down and study until I really had it. I also began to see that if I wanted to get through any course as prescribed, no matter what I thought of the teacher or the subject, I'd better be able to answer the teachers' questions with information as they had put it out.

It was difficult because I wanted the teachers to test me on the questions I had studied in the book—and they never would. I'd get kind of upset with them, too, because they'd always say stuff I wasn't interested in at all, that I didn't want to read about. I would go through it so I was familiar with it, but they would word a test question in a way that I had to know the information, not just be familiar with it.

I was finding out that nothing really is individual or secret or hidden, that it is all an open book that can be read very easily by anyone who cares to take the time. I did this for a long time, and eventually, within two or three minutes of reading a book, I could easily pass the examination with a C, and without reading the book I could at least get a D.

Some other people would read the same thing and get A's and B's. So I was still pretty dumb in this hierarchy of smartness, and I didn't like that because, after all, I grew up with them; we ate the same type of food, went to the same schools, chased around, got in the same type of trouble together. But they'd get A's and B's and I'd get C's and D's—until they started telling me that "if you watch how the professor's doing it, he'll telegraph the information." I started watching, and, sure enough, the professor was telegraphing answers, so I'd just write down the answers. I'd study the answers, take the test, and get an A.

So then I had a lot of time to mess around and do a lot of other things, but I found out I was prejudicing myself just as badly that way as I was the other way because I was missing the things I really wanted in life. I was ending up pleasing a lot of people, which is worshiping the god of opinion—being too concerned about what "they" say and what "they" think—and I kept modifying my responses into the world to please others. I did this until, eventually, I didn't know who was saying, "This is my body, this is my mind, and these are my emotions."

I was trying to get in with certain people, so I was giving answers the way I thought they would give answers, so that word would get back to them that I was talking like them and I'd be one of them. It didn't work. They wanted somebody different, but I didn't know it. I thought they wanted somebody like them so it would be compatible and they would then mold the person to suit themselves. I was fortunate that I didn't get into that particular group, but I didn't feel fortunate at the time. Instead, I felt, "Everything's against me. This is bad; this is terrible." I was busy judging what was going on around me and was so busy judging that I was losing track of who was doing the judging.

My mouth was saying a lot, but it was based upon a feeling and a thought that somebody (me) who was backwards was pushing out. And I never could find out who kept putting their foot in my mouth. I didn't want to say something, but I would, and then it would come back and someone would say to me, "I heard two weeks ago that you said these things." Then I'd try to modify it real fast and say, "Well, what I really meant was this," trying to say it to please that person. Then they would tell somebody else, and that second person would come around and say, "You told so-and-so these things," and then I'd try to modify that to please the person in front of me.

All I was doing was trying to please people so they'd like me—but I never got anybody to like me. They were sure putting up with me, though, because I always felt like I was a trouble-maker.

One day I remember asking myself, "Oh, my God, why did I say that?" The answer was, "You're trying to impress people with something. You want them to look at you." But they weren't doing that and hadn't been doing that, so I figured that there was a darn good chance they wouldn't do it in the future. So I decided to watch the future for a six-month period to see if they would change—but they didn't. But, then, I didn't change either, so I was getting what I was putting out.

All this time, I thought I was really a smart, sharp young individual and that I could perceive precisely what was going on. I had a lot of answers for a lot of things. But I was dumb because all I could do was give the answer. I couldn't live what was going on into a higher consciousness, so I kept perpetrating fraud against myself. Not even wanting to, not even intending to, I'd just open my mouth and out would come this big story, and I'd think, "My God, who's telling the story?" It wasn't the truth or what I knew, but it was so close that I was still getting along pretty well with it.

It was boiling down more and more to the residue left by my continually seeing things in error. My heart seemed to be in the right place—until I started searching it. I found out, "You're afraid people are going to call you on it, and you won't be able to stand up." Then I thought, "All right, I'll let them call me on something, and I'll see if I can stand up." So I just stated something right out, and people said, "It's about time." All the time these people, who were my friends, knew that I was telling them story after story after story after story.

So then I found a whole different group of friends who wouldn't hold me to the line and make me behave. I *thought* these were my friends, and if these were my friends, I didn't need enemies because they were letting me continue a habit.

Finally, I made it a point that "from this time on, no matter how popular or unpopular it is, I will say it if it is my duty to speak, but I won't seek to speak just to talk." So there were many, many weeks when I had very little to say to anybody. And during this time, the emotions settled down, the mind settled down, and the body stopped aching and hurting. Something would say, "Now you're getting smart," and I kept wondering who on earth was saying that. I was still separated from the thing that *is*.

I began seeking out people I felt were wiser than me, who had more knowledge. I found out that they could repeat things out of a book (I could read the book, too), but they couldn't give me an experience that could validate what was written. I had to have the *experience* because I wanted to know for myself.

Eventually, one of them said to me, "If you do this, this, this, and this, then this should happen."

So I did this, this, this, and this, and it took place. I said to myself, "Now I have found someone who can teach me. And if *he* can teach *me, I* can't teach *him,* so I'll shut my mouth and I'll listen." And no matter what the person brought to me, no matter what he said, I would just do it blindly, faithfully. He never could hurt me because I had such loving trust going that there was no way he could violate it. I didn't even know at the time that I had just entered into a clear consciousness.

But I still wasn't getting ahead the way I felt I should. So I asked the person, "Can I ask you a question, because I've listened for so many months?"

The person said, "I expected you to ask questions before this."

"Well," I said, "these questions have been on my mind."

He said to go ahead, so I asked, "Why is it that I'm still having a lot of personal difficulties? When I'm with you, I don't have difficulties, and everything is really smooth and fine and dandy, but when I go back out into the world, I have the difficulties."

He told me, "That that you've created is still coming upon you," and I said, "Thank you."

I didn't know what on earth that meant— "that that you've created is still coming upon you"—but I hadn't understood a lot of things he had said. So I went home and wrote the words on a piece of paper: That that you have created is still coming upon you.

It was about a month or two later when I said, "Could I ask a question?"

He said yes, and I said, "When?"

"All before you met me and before you were born onto this planet this time, all before then, and before then."

I asked, "How far back?" and he said, "Beyond reasoning."

I was ready to pack my tent and leave. I guess I know what it means to have absolutely no ego going. It was like I was pulling my chest in and out to breathe—and I was even wondering who was doing that. The blood, everything, had drained down to the pit of my stomach, I was all cold and shaky, and I knew I couldn't stand up because my legs would have collapsed.

I thought, "How come this person can say that to me and make me have this experience? Why is this person, who I've trusted and loved and respected and learned so much from, doing this to me? He could have done so many other things that would have been so much nicer." Then I thought, "Oh, my God, here I am, back to controlling how he should be."

He just sat there and looked at me, and I must have sat there for anywhere from a half-hour to two days. There was nothing really going on, no thoughts, no questions; all I was doing was circulating blood. At some point I got my strength up, and I just walked out. But I was back very shortly and said, "I'd like to listen again."

He looked at me and said, "One thing you have, and that's guts." (I knew what that meant because I had felt them for weeks, churning inside me.) He also said, "I know you've got blood."

I said, "Yes, I felt that all in one spot down here in my stomach."

He told me, "It's going to take great courage to find truth."

I thought, "Well, that's a very subjective point of view," and immediately I was right back, holding myself against the person who was giving me everything. I was now challenging the teacher.

Then it hit me. I said to myself, "Oh, come on, stop that," and I asked the teacher, "How long do I challenge like this in my mind and go back to this other pattern?"

He said, "Until you learn better."

So I left. I went home and wrote that on a piece of paper: Until you learn better. To me, that was one of the most nebulous statements. I was so far from learning anything that I didn't even know what "better" was going to be when I got there.

The difficulties were very severe because I had the spiritual promise inside me. It was close to the surface; I knew it and I felt it, but nobody could see it. How could they see it? I was throwing too much baloney their way, and they were fed up with it.

So one day I asked the teacher, "Can I ask you a question?" He said no, and tears came all over the place. I don't even know where they came from; it was just tears and tears and tears and tears. He went on talking to other people, like, "Well, go ahead, crybaby," and that made it worse because I wasn't a crybaby. I wouldn't cry if they were going to kill me; I'd say, "Go ahead." But this person could reduce me to tears with a *no*.

Nobody else could move me from my position, and this person wasn't even making any attempt to move me from my position. He was just telling me. And when he'd say something to me, I'd start having experiences. If other people told me the same thing when I'd ask them, nothing happened. Why was this person able to move me with words and give me an experience and the other people were only there? I'd look at them and think, "You're as dumb as I am."

I'd have experiences of judgment, and I began to think, "If they are as dumb as I am, I'm as dumb as they are. And if they're really dumber than I am, then I've got to move into their stupidity with them." And I found out I was locking myself against myself into patterns of lesser and lesser and lesser quality because I was busy trying to equate myself in the physical world with everything around me so that I could feel at one with it. But this kept changing. The seasons would keep changing, the wind would blow, the sun would come out, and sometimes it would do it all at the same time, and I'd be really confused. I could wear a heavy coat against the wind and then roast in the sun.

This was a time when I felt worse than Job in the Bible. I'd think, "The devil was nice to Job, but these things that are happening to me are terrible. I'm really being picked on. And besides that, nobody really cares."

So, when I finally got up my nerve, I went back to this teacher, who, at least, was telling me things. I thought, "Maybe he cares because at least he's *telling* me." Then one day I realized that this person had more love for me in three seconds or in his little finger than I had all day for everything in the world and all week for anything and all year for him.

I was way behind just in the level of love. So I figured, "What will the person who is the super lover do when they are indeed in love and loving?" The answer was, "Anything that has to be done."

So I would start doing things that had to be done. Then there would be people saying,

"You can't do that," and I would feel rejected and hurt. I'd think, "I won't do that for *you* anymore." Then I'd think, "Now, wait a minute. It's 'anything that has to be done,' and that rejection had to be done. So, okay, I'll take it, I'll eat of that." I ate all the humble pie in that town, and I was starting to eat crow.

Then I heard another teacher talking about being divine, and I thought, "That's the last straw. He's divine, and I'm not even anything yet." The person turned to me and said, "You're divine, too," and I thought, "Boy, I could really do something with that if I would like to. I'll run it up the flag pole and see what happens."

So I ran back to my teacher: "Can I ask a question?" He said yes, and I asked, "Am I divine?"

He said, "What do you think?"

Down came the flag.

I went back to the second teacher and said, "I'm not divine. If you're divine and you said

I'm divine and I'm not, then you're not, either, because you made a mistake."

He asked me, "How do you come to this?"

I said, "Well, I asked my teacher, and the teacher asked me what I thought."

He said, "Did he say you weren't divine?"

I said no and thought, "Back to the teacher." Up goes the flag.

So I said to my teacher, "Question."

"What?"

"Is it possible that a human can be divine?" He said yes, and I thought, "That was a good question." I had the first ray of hope after God knows how many years of just going from day to day to day to day and hoping the sun would come up. (One day I even commanded it to come up, and it was right on schedule. The next day I said, "Don't come up," and it came up right on schedule. So, I figured, forget that.

Only command what you can command, and the rest, let it go because it's out of your area.)

I would sit there while the teacher was telling me things, thinking, "Yes, it is possible that you can be divine. It's possible to be divine in a physical body. Now I wonder if that person really is." Then I thought, "Wait a minute. I've entertained doubt before. Would I know if he was or he wasn't? Would I know?" So I thought, "There's only one way to find out and that's to go and see who the person is."

So I left that teacher and went to the second one. I said, "I've left my other teacher to come to you."

He said, "You're stupid."

"Why is that?"

"You doubt your other teacher and you're not sure of me, and so you can never find sureness in yourself. Go back to your other teacher and don't doubt him, but learn everything you can and then come to me."

I thought, "Well, he's rejected me. He's divine, he says he's divine, and I don't know if he is or he isn't. I mean, if he says so, that's fine with me. But now the guy has turned me down, and I'm being rejected by God." That's the ultimate rejection.

So I went back to the first teacher and said, "Question."

"What?"

"Can I come back to the class?"

"No."

I sat there with some vocabulary words going through my head. He turned and looked at me, and he said, "That doesn't do it either."

So I knew vocabulary words wouldn't work. I said, "Question."

"Yes."

"Yes, what?"

"You have met your new teacher."

I said, "That person won't take me."

He said, "That's because you can't see what's going on yet."

I asked, "Do you know him?"

"Yes, that was the person who taught me."

It took a long time, but I gradually started seeing why I was having difficulties. I could start to see the veil lifting off the stage, and I thought, "Pretty soon I'm going to have the light on me, and I'm going to be able to perform." It opened just a little bit, never all the way, but I could see that it was there, though it was a long, long way away from me.

So I went to the class of the second teacher. I didn't say, "Question. Can I come to your class?" Inside me, it was more like, "I'm in your class." He turned around and just looked at me, almost saying, "Look who thinks he's here."

The other teacher wouldn't have me, my friends would lie to me, my enemies would block me, and those who were neutral didn't give a damn, and I couldn't stand that either. I had to have somebody who could hold steady long enough for me to find out what was going on inside.

In the meantime, I was going through a lot of things, like surgery and illnesses. Everybody I was around was having it, too. If I wasn't having it, they were having it, and I was having it right along with them vicariously. My sympathy was running over. Somebody would have a headache, and before you knew it, I was having a headache, too. In fact, I started getting ingrown toenails because my father had them. I figured, "Who needs them? That's his." At this point of saying, "That's his, that's yours, that's yours, that's yours," everything straightened out.

But the person who then started teaching me a great deal never really taught me, never put his arm around me, never said, "Come and sit by my side, come and eat with me, come to my house and visit like the others do." I waited and waited for an invitation, and that guy never gave me one. It's called a carrot, right out in front of the jackass, where you go and you go and you go.

One day I said, "Question." He said yes, and I thought, "I'm in the class!"

He waited—and I'd forgotten the question. I knew what the answer was: dummy. I went to ask a question and was too dumb to ask it, so the answer was "dummy." I wondered how I got that because I never called myself dummy, but that's where I was. I thought, "Gee, if I listen, this man talks on this level, but he does something over here, too." He wasn't stirring me like the first teacher was, but at night this guy was in my dreams. It was like, "God! Will you get out of my dreams? It's enough to be picked on in the class and to be rejected, but who needs all this other stuff?" It was a very subtle type of training, and I had to be increasingly more subtle.

One day I went back to the first teacher's class. I walked in, and he said, "Come," and he sat me in his chair.

I thought, "Oh, my God. What do they want to hear from me?" I said, "I have nothing I can tell you." I saw the room start to get light all over the place, and I thought, "They're going to get it even if I don't say it. And no matter what I say, they're going to get it ... I'll just tell them a joke."

So I told them a joke, and it cracked them up. They were hilarious about it, and I realized that I was brought in there to tell the joke to break up a crystallization in the group. Then we held a meditation and I left. The joke was the whole thing I was there for: I was there to be a joker.

When I thought about it, I wasn't too happy with the idea. I'd much rather have been divine, giving some fantastic message. I'd rather have said, "Hallelujah, brother. Levitate!" I'd like to have told them about all the flying saucers up on the hill that were there waiting. But, by this time, I couldn't tell them a lie because they'd all know it, and I'd go to the back of the class again.

So I went back to my current teacher. I said, "Question," and he said, "I sent you there."

I said, "Question," and he said, "I answered it."

So I said, "Well, no, I didn't ask it yet."

"Ask."

"I went back to the other teacher and told a joke. Why'd I go there?"

He said, "I sent you there."

I thought, "Now, he was just lucky on the answer. He could have said that for just about anything."

And he said, "Don't you believe it."

He had been talking to everybody, and he turned to me and said, "Don't you believe it."

I thought, "But I do believe it. I believe everything he says."

He turned to me and said, "What I say—I tell you the truth. But what you were saying was not the truth."

He went on and I was thinking, "This guy is doing a number on me." It was almost like tick-tack-toe all over my forehead, and he was writing STUPID. I didn't like that, but I'd rather have him write that than nothing at all.

This sort of thing went on for quite a while. Then one day after class, I said, "Would you like to go out and have a cup of coffee?"

He said, "I never thought you'd ask."

I thought, "How long have I been in this class and been rejected and felt rejected and hurt and pushed down—and he's been waiting for me to ask?" I'd been waiting for him to invite *me* over.

So I walked out the door—and forgot to take him. Just forgot all about him. I was out the door, in my car, down the road, into a café, and got a piece of pineapple pie. The waiter asked, "Do you want anything to drink with it?"

I said, "Well, I thought I'd have a cup of... where is he?"

Out the door, in my car, going like gang-busters a few blocks, in the door, and he's sitting there in the chair with his hat on. I said, "Oh, my God!" I started laughing and fell at his feet. My head went on his knee, and I was laughing and laughing, and the tears came. I sat there, and I cried and cried and cried and cried and cried and cried. I guess I cried about fourteen lifetimes—and he said, "Did you pay for your pineapple pie?"

"Oh, my God, no!" I was up and got to the door, and I said, "Do you want to go?" and he was coming right behind me, very fast.

We got in the car, and I went around the corner on one wheel (the steering wheel). We parked the car and went in, and there was my pie sitting there with a check by it, the cup of coffee, and another cup of coffee. I said, "I don't drink coffee. Is somebody sitting there?" They said no, so I sat down, and he sat across from me.

The waitress came and got the coffee and put it in front of him. I picked up the check, and what was really funny is that when I went to pay it, I didn't have any money. I couldn't even leave a penny tip. I was going to leave my watch and come back later to pay it. (I think at that time it was 49¢ for all of that. It seemed to be a real bargain, but the pineapple pie was really terrible.)

I never got around to drinking the coffee. My teacher didn't get around to drinking the coffee, either, but was just with me. And just that he would be there with me solved many things that were not apparent to be solved. They didn't need to be solved. There was nothing to be solved. He was solving it because he was there.

I looked at him and said, "Are you ready to go?"

"No."

A few minutes later, I asked, "Are you ready to go now?"

"No."

I could feel everything getting tight, like, "Let's see. What do I do? Do I get a headache? Do I say I have to go to work? Are they going to close the place pretty soon?" But I knew it was an all-night place, so I couldn't put that on him.

It was about an hour on a piece of pie and a glass of water. The pie went down in about five minutes, and the water went down in about ten, so I sat there and fiddled with the glass for another fifty minutes.

I finally said, "Well?"

He said, "Does it bother you that much to have me with you in public?"

I thought, "Oh, my God. Where am I? I'm back on the same thing that I was doing two years ago, feeding everybody baloney and they all didn't like it. And this person is saying this to me."

I said to him, "Oh, no. No, that's not it. I was afraid that I was inconveniencing you."

He said, "Don't you think I would tell you?"

"Yeah, I *think* you would tell me. But whether you would or not, I'm not too sure."

I could feel myself going to the back of the class real fast. There was something inside me that was leaving, like everything was being shut off, and I said, "I figure in your time you'll do what you do. And I guess in my time I'm going to do what I do. And maybe our time now is to go do something else."

He said, "Well, I'm ready."

I hadn't asked him, "Do you want to go do something else?" I had said, "Are you through?" This is what I was really saying, and he said he wasn't through. Then I realized, "This guy answers the question. He doesn't take my *meaning*; he takes my *question*."

So I said, "Where would you like to go?"

He said, "Down this street, and I'll tell you when to turn."

We went down the street, and he said, "Take a left." I was in the right lane and it was like, "I can't. There are cars there."

We went another block, and I got in the left lane. Another block, and he said, "Go right."

"But you wanted to go left."

This continued for about sixteen blocks. It was about two o'clock in the morning, and there weren't too many people in the road, so I thought, "Ha ha! I got it!" And I drove down half of each lane, the white line right under the car. I came to an intersection and said, "Which way?" and he said straight ahead, so I pulled over into the right lane.

Suddenly I thought, "He's going to say left at this next light, so I'd better find out if there's a car back there." I saw there were no cars back there, so I just oozed over into the left lane. I looked back, no cars in the right lane, and I said, "Which way?"

He said, "Right," and I made a right turn. He asked, "How did you know to do that?"

I said, "I checked to see if there were cars behind me, because I knew you were doing something and I wanted to be prepared."

And he said, "Now you're on your way."

I wanted to be prepared, so I had to watch all the lanes of traffic around me, and this man was giving me a driver's test at 2 o'clock in the morning. I already had a license, but I was after another license: the license to do, the license to follow directions.

He said to me, "Why didn't you turn left the first time?"

"I didn't know."

"Do you think I would run you into something that would hurt you?"

"Well, yeah," I said, "I guess so. That's why I didn't turn."

"Would I?"

I said no, and he said, "But you thought so."

"Yes," I said, "and my actions said that." He asked me to explain. I was driving him home; he mentally took over driving the car, and I just steered it while I explained it to him. When we got to his house, I let him out and said, "I'll see you later."

He said, "You've learned now what I can teach you."

I looked at him for a minute, and then I said, "Okay." No rejection, no question, no recriminations, no "can I do it or can't I do it."

About two months later, I went back to see him. When I went in the room, he said to come and sit up on his chair. I thought, "Oh, my God," and everything inside started going wooooohhhhhh because this man knew every thought in my mind that had been there, that would be there, and that would ever come there.

I sat on the teacher's chair, and somebody said, "Question." I said yes, and they asked a question and back came the answer. Somebody else said, "Question," and I said yes. Those "dummies" asked all the questions that I had been asking all the time, and I had every answer. But I found out they weren't so dumb. I found out that they honest-to-God wanted to know. And this was the question they kept asking me over and over—and it's the same question I hear from people I work with: "How do I make this work? How do I do this?"

That's really the question, even though people phrase it many different ways. The answer is that you must always do it yourself, regardless. No matter what takes place at any time, no matter where, no matter who you're with, you must hold true to that thing that says, "I am that I am." You must always hold to that. It will not think, it will not feel, it will not have a body; it is what it is. That is the part that is divine.

Then when I say, "I am divine," that is not ego, body, or emotions. It is "that that is" saying it because nothing else can say it except that. It *says* that. The rest say, "I feel divine, I think I am divine, I look divine, I'd like them to think I am divine." But the part that says "I am" is the part of God consciousness that resides inside you. That was the awakening to self-realization, to the true self.

The self of one teacher was the level that teacher was going to function on, so then I had to go to the teacher who was going to function in the spiritual level beyond the Soul. These people don't have to be identified, and I think I've paid a great deal of respect to them already. And, eventually, we all say, "Thank God for my guru, my teacher, my leader, my Light bearer, my one who stood by me, the one who really couldn't care less one way or another what I did and if I made it, but all the time was making sure I wouldn't fail. All the time."

When I look back over some of that, especially when someone starts getting nostalgic, I go back to those years of the various jobs I had, the things I was doing, where I was traveling, and the hurt and the turn-down. And I see that each of those things was being guided by those teachers from a higher consciousness *for me,* and I didn't have the wit to know that all along they were watching me go through my little hell. That was the purification, for me to find out all the things that weren't necessary that I thought were necessary so that I knew humble pie from crow (and from pheasant or anything else) and learned that no matter where you are, you must always be that that you are.

This is not seeking somebody to praise you for more than you are or to make you less than you are. It's someone to come to the level you're on, say yes to that level, and then kick you into another level. Sometimes, it's by not inviting you to have dinner with them, by an apparent rejection—and, all along, those people knew exactly what I would do.

I never feel so much like a puppet on a string as I do when I'm talking to people—because I must present the consciousness for the group (which makes me a puppet on a string). And, at the same time, I must maintain who I am so that this part that says, "I am that I am," the divine part that comes through, will hold no matter what you say or think or where you go or what goes on in your mind. It will hold because, whether you're dumb like me and it takes fifteen or twenty years or you're smart like a few who can do it overnight, at the end of that time you'll be sitting on what you want. And even though right now you may not know what you want, that part that you do want will appear and you'll have it and you'll say, "This is what I really, honest to God want, desire, need." It's what you already are, and you've always been that.

Some people look in my eyes and say, "Oh, J-R, I see so much hurt," and I say, "You're seeing accurately. There has been hurt. But look deeper, past that, and you will see the joy, the elation, the thanksgiving that says, 'They didn't take it away from me. They let me walk every step of the way.'"

You can do the things you want to do, but you're responsible for all of it. So you start becoming responsible for your thoughts, your feelings, your body and what you take into it, and your addictive patterns. You move into moderation so that you're not dependent upon this world. Dependency upon anything in this world makes you come back into this world.

And at some point you will enlighten, be born again, awakened to Spirit. The world dies for you, and you walk *on* the world, but you're from the Spirit. At that point, it is spiritual liberation, and then you say, "I never was kicked out of the Garden of Eden. I just closed my eyes."

THE WAYSHOWER

CHAPTER FOUR

My Kingdom
for a Horse

PROBABLY ONE OF THE GREATEST DAN-GERS WE HAVE IN APPROACHING THE SPIRITUAL LIFE IS THE SEEKING FOR RECOGNITION: "RECOGNIZE ME. SEE WHAT I'M DOING."

I can think back over the years to when God in the form of my teacher (who was, indeed, God) would completely ignore me when I would seek to be known by God by way of my teacher. That is really quite screwy because I knew my teacher was omnipotent and omnipresent, in all times and in all things, and yet sought recognition of his physical body. And he'd give me recognition from his physical body and denied me recognition of the spiritual body.

One day in my stupidity, I said, "Why is it that I do not see you?"

He said, "You see me."

I said, "Yes, you let me come to you. I have access to you whenever I want. I can come in and tap you on the shoulder and ask you a thousand questions. And you always turn to me and give to me continuously. Then when I'm not with you, why am I fallow and empty?"

He said, "Well, you wanted this. You wanted recognition in the physical body and you gave up the other."

It really hurt to find out that to go for the recognition of his physical body denied me the divineness, yet I also knew that inside of that physical body resided the divineness. He wasn't hurting me or condemning me or anything like that, and I knew that I was still getting it. But that getting, if it's only present within the physical form, means that someplace along the line something's not working.

It was also quite obvious in that big ashram, that community of thousands of people, that I was as well-known as the teacher. I was revered and, in a sense, worshiped, and I encouraged that. I played on it and played up to it. In fact, I was writing the script; I had complete orchestration of every instrument. My guru would say something, and I'd say, "What he's saying is this." And he'd just sit there and look at it and watch me play the ass. He never labeled me (and I wasn't too smart to label myself).

Then that teacher sent me off to get horses. Getting those horses was six months one way and six months back the other way if I could get them immediately and return. But it was more like four or five years of being away from my teacher. You can't believe the agony I felt over wanting a physical form. Then I thought, "Why would my teacher set himself up that way to destroy me this way?"

My guru was very, very clever. He sent me on this mission of great responsibility, which could go only to his most trusted one, the one who had been found true and had been tested and knew how to think like the guru, who could transact business in his name, his way. It made me feel so joyful to think, "Oh, my God,

I am chosen. I am *the* chosen one to go do this in the name of my guru, who is known around this planet," at least in my head.

After going down the road four or five days on this mission, I realized I had a question to ask my guru. I wanted to go back, but to get there and come back again to keep going, I'd have to be really rushing, riding a high-speed horse to get there to talk to him and then getting on a horse and riding all the next day to get to where the group was, plus how far they'd gone on ahead.

I tried it, believe me. I was so praised for my devotion to my guru and my group that I was riding back hundreds of miles to sit at the feet of my guru and get his darshan and ask him a question, and then to get on a horse and ride all night long to get up to the group of my people to shepherd them on their way, and then, when they were settled for the night, to get back on my horse and ride all that distance back to him. Believe me, that's devotion. Also, it makes for an awfully sore rear end.

I did this for about four weeks until the

physical broke. It broke at the feet of my guru, and I said, "I can't go back."

He called his people and said, "Put him on a stretcher and put him in this carriage and take him back, because he has a job to do and he can't let it down."

"But I'm broken physically. I'm very ill."

He said, "Well, by the time you get to them, you'll be healed enough to resume your responsibilities."

So I went to do that. And the first night there I felt the agony of not being able to go back to see my guru. I was wide awake, thinking, "I'll get on that horse and I'll go. I'll show them." But I couldn't get my rear end up off the cart I was on, so I excused myself: "Well, I would do it if I could, but I can't."

A lot of people around me said, "Why did you break your body down so we have to take care of you so much and we can't do these other things?"

I said, "That was in the service of my guru. Anyway, you *should* do that for me because look what I did. I mean, have you ever seen such devotion? Have you ever seen such an idiot parading? Have you ever seen such a big jackass in your life that you're following?" It was dawning on me.

For almost two years in that sojourn, it was complete agony and despair. And the one I loved above all things made me come to the presentness that if he was omnipotent and omnipresent, then he was there present immediately. But he didn't manifest himself and denied me the spiritual radiation of the spiritual form until I'd eaten the karma of occupying the physical place that belonged to other people. I had to "eat" the space of all the people who would have come to sit there, whom he could have instructed and just have been there with them even if he said, "How are you?" and also talked to a hundred other people. I had denied the spot of their existence out of my stupidity. But through his grace and his love and his absolute devotion to me (which made mine so picayunish it was miserable), he sent me out and had me eat the karma.

While I transacted all the horse trading, I came to the point where I did it anonymously. I said, "I am just a poor, humble servant for a man who asked me to come and do this," and I got the best deals on those horses. If the people had known it was for my guru, the price would probably have been quadrupled because they'd have been able to have had all the publicity: "I sold all these horses to so-and-so, and he paid these prices, so these horses are extremely valuable," and then they'd rip off all the neighbors. And it can't be done.

On the way back to the ashram, I realized I hadn't given my guru credit. I hadn't said who I was doing it for. I hadn't given myself credit. It was a failure that I hadn't transacted the business in the name of my guru.

And it was in that period of time that my guru appeared in the radiant form inside of me. It wasn't just inside of me; it was all around me. It was in the trees, the rocks; it was in the dung of the camels and things like that. It was just all over. And I realized, "Oh, my God. He's all over. He's omnipresent. He's in everything at all times." He was always there, and to ask a question was to be foolish, for the answer was immediately present: "I am here." When I was with him physically I had plied him with these questions of stupidity and ignorance about my own little mundane world, thinking I was devoted to the guru. Yet I had separated him from the reality of being me, and me him—completely separated in stupidity.

It was over two years of going back. And it took longer than that to find out that the grace of the guru was sufficient, that he was who he was, was sufficient, and that I needed nothing else. I became so complacent—not complacent in terms of doing nothing, but that peacefulness and that oneness that I could sleep on a horse, I could sleep in a mud hole, I could sleep with hundreds of other people. It didn't matter because I was always asleep within the consciousness of the Beloved, and that loved one was always present.

You know, it can become very sobering when you have to turn around to the people you've been instructing for a long time and bow at each one's feet—the guru in them—and for them to then take that and throw it back on you and to belittle you. And they had the right to do that. The slings and arrows of outrageous fortune were just a fairy tale compared to the slings and the arrows of people who are vindictively getting you. And you had to let them get you. You didn't want them to get you because it hurt, because someplace inside you the ego was still hanging on to its vested interest: "But when I get back to the guru and I'm welcome there, I'm going to turn around and fire the hell on you people." And I realized that when I got back to the presence of my guru, I would do nothing except what I was doing at the time, and that was being the servant that he sent me to be. He sent me to be his servant, to serve *him* in all things.

The guru would serve people and clean up after them; he did all the things needed. It used to amaze me that he had the energy to do it and answer my questions and be with me to the exclusion of others. But I was the prime example of what a horse's ass was, and he used me as his teaching device. When I was gone he'd say, "You all remember so-and-so."

They'd say, "Oh yeah, do we remember so-and-so."

He'd say, "Don't do what he did. Don't do the devotion like that. Don't come to me like that. Don't do things like that."

I realized that because, while he was teaching them, he would take me into the spirit of his beingness, and I would hear him tell people that. And some part of me would feel the wrongness of what I had done, the error, the spirit of error that I'd entertained under the guise of knowing and being smart.

But I couldn't pick anybody up with my spiritual body and take them. I'd said I could. I'd lied. I tried to get them to believe I could. It wasn't true. And I had to confess all the errors of spirit. I couldn't just say, "Look, I lied to you all along." I had to come to each one and say, "All those times when I said this and this," and give all the details. And they'd say, "You what? Oh, my God!" It was my telling them the truth that was destroying them, and I had to eat the karma of the destruction of myself and the destruction of them. But it was all being done perfectly through the guru, the master teacher.

And we all entered into fellowship, that when we finally brought the horses back into this community, there was just joy among us. We were singing; the horses were singing. They were neighing. They had their heads up high, their tails were pointing up in the air, their manes were flowing, and there was music going out all over. We were yelling out our songs of love to people, that there was a oneness coming in.

Then I thought of Jesus' triumphal entry into Jerusalem, and I thought, "Hey, that was really similar." Then I thought, "Watch it that you do not falsely identify and curse yourself with your mouth."

And I said that the guru was great. But the Bible says, "Greater is he that is in you, than he that is in the world" (1 John 4:4). My guru was in the world, but the guru that was in me was the very spiritual form. And it became very interesting that that type of attitude—like falling prostrate to the guru inside of you—kept you from wrongdoing, kept you in a state of joy even if at times you had to work your karma.

I used to say, "Well, why don't you just take the karma from me?" and my guru would say, "That I'm here is sufficient." I never could understand that and would think, "I know you're here and I know that's sufficient, but why don't you take it? Why do I have to do that? Why do I have to lose my loved ones? Why do I have to go through this hell and agony?"

And he'd say, "Because I'm here, that's sufficient," which to me was such a Pollyanna-ish cop-out until he demonstrated that he was, indeed, here, and I knew that no matter what happened, that was sufficient. The people would come and go. They'd call you names, and that the guru was there was sufficient for them to call those names and do anything they wanted to.

It was amazing how before, when things would get bad, I would think, "Oh, God, this is *bad,*" and after the guru made his presence known to me in all things, things got worse. The horses would get sick. I thought the most expensive stud was going to lose its reproductive system, and I was worried and upset. Things were bad, and I thought, "Oh, God, why did you send me on this trip? I can't do this. I'm the least one you should have sent. I'm not a veterinarian. I'm just a guy who can ask questions and cuddle up to my guru and take other people's space and profess great devotion, great love, and great oneness. I'm too smart." My teacher let me, and that's when you really get taught.

When we entered into the city and everybody took the horses to the guru, I went to my little humble place and got cleaned up and was preparing a record to give to my guru when he asked for it. And he came in to where I lived. You know, when you see the radiance of him in the inner and you see the outer, the outer is nothing. And so immediately you forget that and say, "Why have you come here to me?

Why are you here? I was going to come to you. Why did you come to me?"

He said, "The reason I came to you is because, before, you never gave me the chance to. You always came to me first. Often I wanted to come *here* and eat food with you *here* and talk to you *here* and be with you *here*, and you kept going *there.*"

He was telling me he was always there, always in my home, and I was always leaving the home to go someplace else to try to be with something that wasn't there. (Yet, of course, it was there.)

Then he would say to me, "Your wife and your children are more devoted to me than you because they stayed here and took care of all the things around you that you neglected."

It gets to be really hard to think that the great spiritual mighty one, which I called myself, was less than the least of his children and less than his wife. (And at that time, that would not be saying anything very good because, then, your horses came before your wife, and even the goat came before her.)

With that, the last part of the ego just died. And when that died, something interesting happened. The emotions of the world, my extension into the world, died also. But the emotions then turned and moved right back in, and the emotions of my Soul, my spirit, met me, and I was blissed out. There's no way to explain it. I was absolutely intoxicated; didn't even know enough to rip off clothes and go roll in the mud or I would have done that; didn't know enough to get up; didn't know enough to do anything, but that my guru was present was sufficient.

It was amazing how there were no problems, there were no difficulties, there were no catastrophes. If there was famine, there was no famine, because that was the time we fasted and got well and got rid of illnesses from living off the fat of the land. When there were no jobs, it was the time for us to go and help other people. When there was nothing of this, there was always that thing that was entirely present that was the divine perfection (not my interpretation). And then entering into the bliss is very easy. It's very easy to see the divineness and the perfection.

Then my guru said, "Now you have to get up and work," and he pulled the bliss back. I thought, "Oh! Not that, not that!" It was like my sugar bottle: "Now I'm going to cry again. Shove it back in my mouth, keep me complacent, keep me quiet." He never did.

That same thing is present today. The form changes, but the formless never does. It's always been there "smacking" you in the head. It's always been there showing its method, its mechanism. The path of the Travelers is not a path of man. Man cannot travel that path. It's a path of God. And only those who are in God can travel that path. So you have to go to that one that is greater inside of you.

That is what we call the Christ, or the Divine, or the Beloved, or the oneness. We have it in here, and sometimes we surround it and defend it against everything, but that defense is also a prison. So we've got to beat down the barriers of our protection and actually leave ourselves infinitely vulnerable—not to our emotions or our mind, but so that this one who is in us can walk in the world. When you do, it's alive inside of you and you have eternal life because you are then alive. You're not in a state of existence. Rocks exist, plants exist, clouds exist. But you're in a state of aliveness, and that aliveness is a state of awareness. It's not a state of doingness, because you don't have to *do* anything. It's a state of beingness: that you're there is sufficient.

There are many people who will just be, and that will be sufficient for them. Our work then cuts itself out for us and we just get to identify it. But if our work is only for ourselves, we fall even in the midst of sitting on the throne. And if our work is for others and all things, even if it's being out in the barnyard with a tin bill on our head, we're doing it in God's kingdom.

To be the very least in the kingdom is to be higher than anywhere else when you're truly just giving and letting it flow and letting the oneness present itself—not as a mechanism of the mind, where you think, "I'm going to do this, I'm going to do that." That's scheming and manipulating. But it is the spontaneity of the nowness of the divineness.

We must always watch; there's not a moment where we cannot watch. We can enter into awareness. We can search ourselves in despair and separation, the inharmonious situations inside of us. But when we find the Traveler is there, that's sufficient. So we can search in a calmness: "Yeah, I'm being turned in a 360-degree circle. That's out of line? Okay. This is out of line? Okay." It's not, "Yeah, but, Lord, because ..." because that's the egoic manifestation. No defense. No attack. Just identification.

THE WAYSHOWER

CHAPTER FIVE

THE MASTER AND
THE MUDHOLE

I REMEMBER ONE LIFETIME WHEN I WAS BEING TESTED BY SPIRIT.

In that life, people would say to me, "You really have everything. You are part of this spiritual path, and things are nice."

I said, "Yeah, it really *is* nice," and suddenly it all started being taken away from me. Transportation went, friends went, all the loved ones went. Job's situation in the Bible was easy because he knew the Lord was involved in it. I didn't know. Job knew he was being plagued by the devil; I hadn't seen him yet. It's easier when you know what it is. When you don't know, it can be "hell."

I fought tooth and toenail against people who tried to take my loved ones from me, hitting them in the head with all sorts of paraphernalia: "Leave my loved ones alone!" Those people just took my loved ones anyway. I'd hit them again, and they'd take the things out of my hand and hit *me* with them. I'd think, "That's not fair." They'd hit me again—and I'd get out of the way. They were just telling me, "You're not going to be able to take it with you, buddy, and don't forget it. And here's a lump for good measure."

So everything was taken from me—everything. The nice thing is that it didn't cost a lot for clothing because it didn't take much to cover me. I also remember when all the clothing was gone. At nighttime I'd go to find a mudhole and put mud on myself so it would dry and keep me warm at night. Then in the daytime I had to get up soon enough to get the mud off so I wouldn't be baked in it. I used to spend a lot of my time looking for a nice mudhole, to get some clean clothing. I also learned that if you put on mud that has lumps and other things in it, it hurts your skin when you put it on.

At times, though, I enjoyed putting that mud on. I was taking the mud and caking it and watching the different designs I could make that would make it really work. But forget it; it wouldn't work for long. If the mud has dried, as soon as you stretch a little bit, it cracks and falls off, and that's a cold spot. Then it hurts to put on cold mud at nighttime, so it's best not to, believe me.

I couldn't work or get work, and I couldn't have anybody help me because I was the scourge, the outcast. Most people wouldn't talk to me and would leave me alone. And there was no one who would take me in.

I was even fighting the dogs for scraps of food and losing regularly. And, eventually, to eat food would make me sick because there was no stomach to hold the food. I would chew it up and spit out what I could because there was nothing there. Digestion, constipation—I didn't have to worry about those things because there was nothing going in except a little mud once in a while. It had some minerals and a few other things in it, like a lot of viruses and bacteria and a lot of droppings from animals.

There was only one thing I would keep saying over and over, and that was the Lord's name. People would tell me to get out of the way so they could run their cattle through the mudholes to get flies off them and to put mud on them so the flies wouldn't bite them. I would keep saying the Lord's name over and over and over, so they called me that.

That went on for a long, long time, going from mudhole to mudhole. Learning to live like that, at the level of just breathing in and breathing out, is called survival.

People would sometimes come to me and say, "You know, you had so much and it's all been taken from you. What did you do wrong?"

I said, "I don't know if whatever it was, was wrong. But I do know that there is no way they can break me, because it's all being done *for* me even in my ignorance."

Even in the ignorance of not knowing and the ignorance of the whole situation, I would not blaspheme God or anybody around me. And I would not say, "Look, Lord. Other people have all these camels and horses and wagons and all this food, and I've got nothing. Why them? Why not me?"

I lived a long, long time in that kind of condition, and some people would ask me, "Why are you so happy?"

I said, "If this is the worst that can happen to me, if this is the worst that they've got to show me, they might as well stop because I'm not going to give up no matter what Spirit, or God, or anybody else does."

They said, "Maybe it's black magic or witchcraft."

I said, "I don't care. If that is the worst they can do, they are shot down."

Was that being an optimist? It was either that or be a pessimist, but why be a pessimist? I was as low as I could go. There was only one way for me to look, and that was up because I was lying down on my back all the time. Everything was truly looking up. And to get up was often a waste of time because I would be back down as soon as I got up, just from having no strength.

One day, I said, "I don't know how long I'm going to be here, but if you are going to keep me here for a long time, that's fine. And if this is what you want to do, that's fine. Whatever you do, that's fine, so go ahead and do it because you are going to do it anyway, and there's nothing I can do."

Then it said, "You endured it."

I asked, "Is that the end?"

They said, "No, but you endured the end of *this*."

And within a period of three or four days, monies that had been owed to me, and things that had been taken from me were being returned to me. I would look at the people and say, "I have no need for this. Give it to others. I have my mud and my mudhole. Why do I need all this that you're trying to give to me?"

It amazed them that I gave away those things and also gave away riches. I did move to a little better situation because winter was coming, and there is such a thing as being practical.

And I don't mean for anybody to try to prove something by going around naked, because they'll throw you in jail. I'm not saying to prove something by not eating. But I am saying that the worst thing that could happen to you is nothing because you will exist, though you might think it is at a level where you couldn't do it.

In that lifetime, pigs were the lowest form, and I'd move them over or try to cuddle up close to get some body warmth. Some people now are sitting in the lap of luxury in this world, and if they don't eat three meals a day, they complain. If somebody doesn't recognize them immediately, they feel resentful. And if others don't recognize them for the great light that's inside them, they think those people must be devils or something like that, and that's not so at all. A lot of the people who are sitting in high places now will be pulled down, and they will get to "wallow with the pigs." I hope they can handle that as well as they can handle the glory they are sitting in now because it must all be treated equally.

That becomes one of the hardest things to do: to take success and failure equally. People come to me and say, "J-R, I really love you; I know who you are," and I say, "Okay. Next." Somebody else comes up and says, "I really doubt who you are," and I say, "Okay. Next." They ask me if it makes any difference, and I say, "None. It's in *you*. It's not in me."

This planet is the "crazy house." There is nobody here who is sane; if they were, they'd leave. But when you can leave your body in consciousness and just walk your body through this level, that's when it really tastes nice. That's having your cake and eating it, too. That's being able to have everything in the world that you want, and want nothing. Then it doesn't matter inside you whether a person says hello to you or never sees you again, because they are part of the process of purifying you.

You can make your hell, your animosity, inside of you by your whole approach to what you think life should give to you. The old adage that "life owes you a living" is nonsense. It owes you absolutely nothing.

And Spirit owes you nothing. You must take from It, but you can't take in a consciousness of poverty. It states in the Bible that man was created to have dominion over all things (Genesis 1). But first you must be a "man," a human, and that's a very beautiful thing to be. This is not an animal masquerading in the human form. It is being that one who can truly handle whatever comes their way, even the mudholes.

THE WAYSHOWER

CHAPTER SIX

COMING INTO THE
TRAVELER CONSCIOUSNESS

IN MY TWENTIES, I HAD TWO MAJOR SURGERIES FOR GROWTHS ON MY FACE AND EYES.

In the midst of the surgery, I realized that I was watching the surgery take place from an entirely different level. I knew that I was unconscious to the physical level, but I was very, very conscious on another level, and the part of me that watched and observed the action was a totally loving, benevolent, fantastic consciousness. That consciousness was the one that I really wanted to be in—totally and in every way. That was the me that I wanted to be consciously aware of and that I wanted to be present always. Within myself, I said that I would sacrifice everything to have that loving consciousness entirely present. I wanted it so badly that I was willing to give up everything if I could just be that and know that, continually, every day. To have that loving, joyous feeling, to have that complete attunement, to know that oneness that never ends—that would be worth everything.

I recovered from the surgery, the years went by, and nothing much seemed to happen. But the path had been set, and my life became one of doing those things that I knew were right to do. I did those things that I knew in my heart were right. And I did right, not for the reward, but just for the sake of doing right. I brought my body into a discipline of understanding. When challenges appeared, I did not know if I could meet them, but I did. I learned many things, took risks, moved into new areas of learning, took on all that I could, and did everything as perfectly and as lovingly as possible.

One night I went to bed and said, "Whoever you are up there, I think it's time. What do you think?" That night I was lifted out of my body and found myself looking down at my own body and everything else. And I realized that the only way to truly know this physical level is to lift up out of it and perceive it clearly from that higher level. It was magnificent.

When I went back into the body, into the physical consciousness, I said, "I have just one request: that I can do this often and get in and out of the body whenever I need to. And whatever I have to do, I'll do." The spiritual forces who were my guides and teachers granted that request, and I started practicing. Sometimes it was difficult; the body would go very rigid and stiff, and everything would go completely asleep. I would come back in the body and realize that I could not make any part of it move. Sometimes I would have to call on the higher forces to help me. I would concentrate on the Christ Jesus, who was my reference point, and ask for his power to move my hand—and it would move. I believed in that, and so it was demonstrated to me. In time and with greater practice, awareness, and ability, I became more adept at going in and out of the body, and as I gained experience in out-of-body travel, I reached into the Soul and learned how to hold and maintain the energy of that realm.

Then in December 1963, I underwent a tremendous transition and was brought into the consciousness of the Mystical Traveler, a consciousness that is totally alive, totally dedicated, totally devoted to the supreme power that is God, that is life, that is love. In retrospect I knew that it was the Traveler Consciousness that had pulled me out of the water when I had the cramp, seen me through car accidents, and walked with me through lies and deceits, through agony and pain, knowing full well that I was going to come out perfect in Soul consciousness.

Now, looking back at the time that I first came into the Mystical Traveler Consciousness, I can realize that my best qualification was that I knew how to love—and, Lord, did I know how to do that! I might not have known how to use my mind too well or my emotions too well, but I did know how to love. I really found it difficult in those early years to try to explain from the intellect what was a heartfelt process. I would try to come up with words that would say what I knew to be so, and I would end up using sign language, but I would still miss the meaning. Then people would say, "How can we get it if you don't explain it?" So I would show them and let them experience the spiritual love, and they would say, "Well, I got that, but that's not what you said."

I would say, "Okay, you tell me what it is." Then I would listen very closely to their words, thinking that they could help me out with some new vocabulary. They would get through talking, and I would say, "That isn't it." But over the years, I have gotten better and better at it, although I still recognize that whenever I attempt to tell you of the Spirit, I miss. There just doesn't seem to be a way to get the Spirit into our vocabulary.

It took quite some time for me to learn to handle the greater energies that were present with my consciousness. When I was seeing spiritually, it was often hard for me to see physically, and I spent a couple of years just learning how to walk so the walls would not "reach out and grab me." They didn't look solid to me, the way I was seeing, but they were solid to my physical body. Or I might be saying hello to someone, reach out to shake his hand, and hit his arm. I would laugh and apologize; there was not too much else I could do at that point. But my sincere message of God and the experience of God was in danger of getting disregarded because people tend to focus on the outer aspects of form.

Those difficulties in handling the energy of Spirit were smoothed out in time, and as the years went by, I learned to demonstrate very dynamically the power of the Spirit, the knowledge and the abilities that are present all the time. This started to revolutionize people's lives. I would write a letter to someone, and there would be so much power with that letter that the print would seem to jump off the paper. It was a demonstration of the power of the Spirit, the Traveler Consciousness, the Holy Spirit, that which is.

THE WAYSHOWER

CHAPTER SEVEN

WORKING WITH PEOPLE

PEOPLE ASKED TO KNOW MORE ABOUT THIS SPIRIT THAT WAS PRESENT.

So I started lecturing a little bit here and there. People began asking more and more for me to talk with them. I knew I did not want a crowd, a group, a following. I just wanted to do what I had to do and to get free of this level without creating havoc. A lot of spiritual teachers, if they are not careful, end up creating a lot more hell than heaven, and I did not want to do that. I have been careful. I have done the work, but I have watched very carefully for the guidance of Spirit all along the way. It is rare that I even get out of bed unless I have a clear directive from the spiritual forces that work with me. I wait until I have the clearance before I even move.

One time, years ago, I was lying in bed and said, "Lord, I'm not moving from this bed until there's a direct okay from You. No messengers. This has to be something that is definitely a process independent of me."

The answer I heard was, "There are no processes independent of you. Don't be a fool." So I got out of bed.

The rest of the message was that I had all the keys, the blessing had been given, and the responsibility was to take care of the people who would come to me because every one is brought by the Father, and those who step into the consciousness of love and who follow the Light and the Sound of God will be returned to Spirit. All have been charged and all are known to God. The directive was laid out very clearly and is now being fulfilled in very beautiful ways.

After holding the Mystical Traveler Consciousness for several years, I completed what I had contracted to do here. The time that I had agreed to serve was up, and I was making preparations to go back to where I live in

Spirit. Then the forces that I work with closely informed me that the ones who were being
trained to become the Traveler had defaulted,
and I thought, "Why me? Why now?"

Their response was, "That's just the way
it is." Also at that time, other spiritual lead-
ers were leaving the planet and leaving their
groups without a focus of spiritual energy
through which to function. So it was suggested by the spiritual forces that I might like to
keep on and function as a battery of power for
these other groups, even though I would still
be working specifically through the Movement
of Spiritual Inner Awareness. So in the end, I
agreed to continue and to work with people
here in the best way that I could.

My job is really quite simple. I love and
I stir people into the awakening of the Spirit
within, and I act as a wayshower as people
move on their spiritual path towards Soul consciousness.

I thought that this whole action would be
enhanced if I found others who could assist me

in this work, so I started looking around for ways to train people to do what I could do. I asked for some assistance and was sent angels. I thought, "What can angels do? Angels are unreal here. Couldn't I have a master or two?"

But the forces said, "Masters won't work with you because they're masters."

I said, "Could I have some apprentices? Could I have somebody that can do this, because if I can get someone else to do this, I can just sit back and channel energy, which is what I do best. I can do a lot of things that I enjoy and then, every now and then, I can focus in on the action, just enough to keep the energy flowing."

Their response was, "Don't get cute."

I said, "That's just the way I am, and for better or for worse, you've got me. And by the way, you said that I have all spiritual authority, so you can't tell me what to do." I made it clear that I was not in a state of rebellion, but rather in a high state of cooperation to find out what was happening. But I found out, as I always find out, that the point of view and the requests expressed by the high spiritual forces are always right and proper, that there is nothing to do but to flow with what is, and that to be of service to Spirit is a blessing beyond all words.

My joy in working with people is in watching them move into their joy, their truth, and their loving center, because that is me, too. That place inside of them that wants it perfect and right and loving is that same place inside of me that has awakened to the perfection that is Spirit, that is Soul.

For so many years there was a part of me that resisted the spiritual flow and said, "I don't want to do that," and I beat up on that part. I said to it, "I don't care what you want to do or don't want to do," and in its hurt, it would say, "I don't want to talk to them. I don't want to confront them. I don't want to do that. I don't want ..." Eventually I found out that, more than anything else, I didn't want to beat up that place inside, so I said, "Okay, it's all right that you don't want to be with people, confront them, work with them, talk with them, but I'm not going to pay a whole lot of attention to you. I'm not going to beat you up, but I'm just going to go ahead and do what I have to do. If you'd like to come along, that's fine, but if you don't, just don't get in the way. I can put you on 'hold' and override you if I have to." And that's what I sometimes did.

That part is still there, and I still hear it every now and then. Some days I give in to that, stay away from people, read my mail, and feel really good about that. Other days, when I have other work to do, I just go ahead and do whatever it is that Spirit directs me to do. I keep the center flowing and let everything live around the work that has to be done. I am living free, and I do not let those childish parts of me run my life or my love. I just am love, and that love runs me perfectly because that love is God.

For those of us who know that we are of God, the responsibility is to live in love and to be loving in all that we do. By our consciousness, we can lift the planet, just by being present and by the energy of Spirit that is manifest through us.

THE WAYSHOWER
CHAPTER EIGHT

How MSIA
Got Started

AS I DID MORE OF THE SPIRITUAL WORK, I TALKED TO INDIVIDUALS AND TOLD THEM WHAT I SAW ABOUT THEIR SPIRITUAL PATH AND KARMA.

As more and more people wanted to talk to me, I got busier and busier. Eventually, in 1968, I was invited to speak to some people in Santa Barbara, California, and that was the beginning of seminars, where I would talk to groups and share what the Spirit brought forward for me to tell them.

I remember one person asking me what we did at seminars. I said, "Well, we're moving the spiritual inner awareness." The person said, "So this is a movement of spiritual inner awareness?" and I said, "Well, sure, that's what it is." In January 1971, The Church of the Movement of Spiritual

Inner Awareness was incorporated. This work kept expanding and taking more of my time, and I started doing it full-time in December 1971.

All the time, I have told people to listen carefully to what I say. Do not believe it. Check it out for yourself. Maybe this path of Soul Transcendence is not for you; there may be many other paths that you have to undergo. People have many strange karmas to fulfill. The Spirit moves people in and out of this Movement of Spiritual Inner Awareness. That is why when new people come in, I say, "Hello," and when people leave, I say, "Good-bye." It is equally the same, and it makes no difference to me.

I thought at first that being the Traveler would be a sign of absolute perfection. And it actually was, but the perfection is not on this physical level; it is on the spiritual levels. Then I started seeing this consciousness unfold in other people. When I would talk to somebody, I would see that consciousness come up inside of them, something would connect, and I started honoring that Spirit in people.

I started seeing other things appear in people—the Christ, the messianic energy. I saw the Holy Spirit; I saw God. I saw things that, if I told you, you would probably say I was absolutely crazy. Well, all the teachings might have seemed "crazy" until they worked for you or you worked them. Then you probably said, "That's not crazy; that's practical."

The levels you are going to go into will sometimes seem crazy to you just because you are new at experiencing them. The levels you are already on are very practical, and you are teaching them to people who are coming up as your "students." You have to be very, very "crazy" to see the face of God. It takes a lot of courage — physical, emotional, and mental courage.

So be who you are. Be Spirit's gift to yourself. Be your own Beloved. Nourish yourself in your awareness of Spirit. And know that you are, as I am, as everyone is, a perfect manifestation of the presence of God.

GLOSSARY

BELOVED. The Soul; the God within.

FALSE SELF. Can be thought of as the ego, the individualized personality that incorrectly perceives itself to be fundamentally separated from others and God.

HOLY SPIRIT. The positive energy of Light and Sound that comes from the Supreme God. The life force that sustains everything in all creation. Often uses the magnetic Light through which to work on the psychic, material realms. Works only for the highest good. Is the third part of the Trinity or Godhead.

KARMA. The law of cause and effect: as you sow, so shall you reap. The responsibility of each person for his or her actions. The law that directs and sometimes dominates a being's physical existence.

LIGHT. The energy of Spirit that pervades all realms of existence. Also refers to the Light of the Holy Spirit.

MAGNETIC LIGHT. The Light of God that functions in the psychic, material realms. Not as high as the Light of the Holy Spirit, and does not necessarily function for the highest good. See also Light and Holy Spirit.

MOVEMENT OF SPIRITUAL INNER AWARENESS (MSIA).
An organization whose major focus is to bring people into an awareness of Soul Transcendence. John-Roger is the founder.

MYSTICAL TRAVELER CONSCIOUSNESS. An energy from the highest source of Light and Sound whose spiritual directive on Earth is awakening people to the awareness of the Soul. This consciousness always exists on the planet through a physical form.

SEMINAR. A talk given by John-Roger or John Morton; also, an audiotape, CD, videotape, or DVD of a talk either of them has given.

SOUL. The extension of God individualized within each human being. The basic element of human existence, forever connected to God. The indwelling Christ, the God within.

SOUL CONSCIOUSNESS. A positive state of being. Once a person is established in Soul consciousness, he or she need no longer be bound or influenced by the lower levels of Light.

SOUL REALM. The realm above the etheric realm. The first of the positive realms and the true home of the Soul. The first level where the Soul is consciously aware of its true nature, its pure beingness, its oneness with God.

SOUL TRANSCENDENCE. The process of moving the consciousness beyond the psychic, material realms and into the Soul realm and beyond.

SPIRIT. The essence of creation. Infinite and eternal.

Additional Resources
and Study Materials
By John-Roger, D.S.S.

BOOK:
FULFILLING YOUR SPIRITUAL PROMISE
If you ever had a question for John-Roger, chances are you'll find it answered here.

This three-volume set of books by Dr. John-Roger is a compendium of information he has shared over many years. Along with an index that makes finding topics easy, its 24 chapters include a wealth of information on subjects including karma, the Mystical Traveler, initiation, and dreams, as well as attitude, relationships, health, and practical spirituality. And at just $45 for the whole set, this resource is a great buy.
Hardbound, 3-book set
ISBN: 978-1-893020-17-7, $45.00

AUDIO:
THE WAYSHOWER
In this four seminar CD packet, you can hear directly from John-Roger the stories of his spiritual journey that inspired this book. The seminars in-

clude: The Search for a Master; The Master and the Mudhole; My Kingdom for a Horse; and The True Self. The stories are funny and poignant; leading up to the profound message of the spiritual work John-Roger is here to do.

Listening to J-R's personal stories of his quest is inspiring, whether you have been on a spiritual path for a while or are new to inner spiritual experiences.

4-CD packet - #3901-CD, $25

SOUL AWARENESS DISCOURSES—A COURSE IN SOUL TRANSCENDENCE

Soul Awareness Discourses are designed to teach Soul Transcendence, which is becoming aware of yourself as a Soul and as one with God, not as a theory, but as a living reality. They are for people who want a consistent, time-proven approach to their spiritual unfoldment.

A set of Soul Awareness Discourses consists of 12 booklets, one to study and contemplate each month of the year. As you read each Discourse, you can activate an awareness of your Divine essence and deepen your relationship with God.

Spiritual in essence, Discourses are compatible with religious beliefs you might hold. In fact, most people find that Discourses support the experience of whatever path, philosophy, or religion (if any) they choose to follow. Simply put, Discourses are about eternal truths and the wisdom of the heart.

The first year of Discourses addresses topics ranging from creating success in the world to working hand-in-hand with Spirit.

A yearly set of Discourses is regularly $100. MSIA is offering the first year of Discourses at an introductory price of $50. Discourses come with a full, no-questions-asked, money-back guarantee. If at any time you decide this course of study is not right for you, simply return it, and you will promptly receive a full refund.

To order John-Roger's books, Discourses, or audio and video materials, contact MSIA at 1-800-899-2665, order@msia.org, or simply visit the online store at www.msia.org

ABOUT THE AUTHOR

John-Roger, DSS

A teacher and lecturer of international stature, John-Roger is an inspiration in the lives of many people around the world. For over four decades, his wisdom, humor, common sense, and love have helped people to discover the Spirit within themselves and find health, peace, and prosperity.

With two co-authored books on the *New York Times* Bestseller List to his credit, and more than four dozen self-help books and audio albums, John-Roger offers extraordinary insights on a wide range of topics. He is the founder and spiritual adviser of the non-denominational Church of the Movement of Spiritual Inner Awareness (MSIA), which focuses on Soul Transcendence; founder, first president, and now chancellor of the University of Santa Monica; founder and chancellor of Peace Theological Seminary & College of Philosophy; chancellor of Insight University; and founder and spiritual adviser of both the Institute for Individual and World Peace and the Heartfelt Foundation.

John-Roger has given over 6,000 lectures and seminars worldwide, many of which are televised nationally on his cable program, "That Which Is," through the Network of Wisdoms. He has appeared on numerous radio and television shows and has been a featured guest on "Larry King Live." He also co-wrote and co-produced the movies *Spiritual Warriors* and *The Wayshower*.

An educator and minister by profession, John-Roger continues to transform lives by educating people in the wisdom of the spiritual heart.

For more information about John-Roger, you may also visit: www.john-roger.org

JSU
GARCIA
PETER
STORMARE
SALLY
KIRKLAND
WITH ERIC
ROBERTS

THE
WAYSHOWER

SCOTT J·R PRODUCTIONS PRESENTS "THE WAYSHOWER" STARRING JSU GARCIA · PETER STORMARE · SALLY KIRKLAND · SEBASTIAN BARR · HOWARD LAZAR · NINA BERGMAN · TOB HUNTINGTON · EVAN HART · RICK OJEDA · ELIZA ROBERTS WITH ERIC ROBERTS PRODUCED REEB JOHNS EDITED MATT RUNDELL MUSIC WARREN WORKMAN COSTUMES LARRY SEYMOUR PRODUCTION REUBEN STEINBERG WRITTEN RICK OJEDA · DAVID HINKINS · LAURIE LERNER STORY JSU GARCIA, DSS & JOHN-ROGER, DSS PRODUCED JOHN-ROGER, DSS DIRECTED JSU GARCIA, DSS & JOHN-ROGER, DSS

A traveler through the ages.

Official Selection
FirstGlance
Film Festival

Official Selection
On Location: Memphis
International
Film & Music Fest

DOLBY
IN SELECTED THEATRES

www.thewayshower.com   www.twitter.com/wayshowermovie   www.facebook.com/thewayshowermovie

THE INSPIRATION FOR THE MOTION PICTURE "THE WAYSHOWER"

The life of Dr. John-Roger, including the specific stories outlined in this book, has inspired the making of a motion picture also titled *The Wayshower.* John-Roger and Jsu Garcia co-wrote and co-directed *The Wayshower* together, and the film was completed in 2011.

The Wayshower stars Academy Award nominee Eric Roberts *(Runaway Train)*, SAG nominee Peter Stormare *(Chocolat)*, Jsu Garcia *(Atlas Shrugged)*, Evan Hart *(Law Abiding Citizen)*, Emmy winner Leigh Taylor-Young *(Picket Fences)*, with Academy Award Nominee Sally Kirkland *(Anna)*, and introducing Howard Lazar *(Freedom to Choose)* and Denmark's TV celebrity and rock star Nina Bergman.

PRODUCTION HIGHLIGHTS

The Wayshower was filmed mostly in Utah, USA, with scenes from filming on location in Morocco, France, England, Peru, and Spain. The metaphysical and abstract nature of many of the elements of this movie have created opportunities for cutting edge sound and visual effects, implemented to further tell elements of the story that are not purely a visual phenomena. With sound from Academy Award Winning Sound Designer Dane Davis *(The Matrix)*, this movie pushes the envelope with the dramatic depiction of supernatural phenomena via sound and effects.

The editing style used throughout the movie creates an artistic, intelligent, and thought-provoking experience for the audience. Just as *The Limey* and *Memento* brought audiences to new levels of involvement and relationship with the story through their unique and non-linear editing, *The Wayshower* similarly presents a new experience for audiences. Steven Soderbergh's influence became both inspiration and support for taking risks with experimental and non-traditional ideas of editing, story-telling, and filmmaking.

Finally, *The Wayshower* presents audiences with questions, and a unique experience and journey with which to fully explore and discover their own answers.

RELEASE AND SCREENINGS

The Wayshower movie has currently screened only in preview screenings to audiences in Los

Angeles, London, and Paris, and has screened across Utah in preview screenings to thank and appreciate local cast, crew, and the communities that helped make this film (Park City, Salt Lake City, Price, Helper, and Moab).

At the time of publication, *The Wayshower* movie has not been officially released. You can keep in touch with the release of this movie and find out about upcoming screenings around the world by joining "The Wayshower Mailing List" at: **thewayshower.com.** You can also see the trailer, read our blog, reviews, and press articles, and see exclusive "behind the scenes" photos and video footage.

You can also keep in touch with *The Way-shower* movie's events, screenings, and updates by connecting with us on:

facebook.com/thewayshowermovie
twitter.com/wayshowermovie

FESTIVALS AND AWARDS

The Wayshower won Best Ensemble Cast at the FirstGlance Film Festival in Hollywood, April 2011, and was also a feature film winner at the Honolulu Film Awards, May 2011.

FOR THE PRESS

Contact Zoe Golightly, 323-422-0002, zoe@msia.org for current information regarding *The Wayshower* movie.

TESTIMONIALS FOR THE WAYSHOWER

"It's the greatest movie I have ever seen."
—*David Wynne, renowned British sculptor*

"*The Wayshower* is a compelling, multi-layered, and complex spiritual journey about a guilt-ridden man searching to understand his connection to his guru J-R. Followers of the real-life guru, John-Roger, as well as a segment of new-thought seekers, will resonate with the messages and life lessons shared throughout."
—*Arielle Ford, author of The Soulmate Secret*

"We absolutely loved *The Wayshower*. It is a very realistic portrayal of a troubled person in search of peace, while at the same time, providing historical information pertaining to one of the most inspirational spiritual teachers alive today."
—*Drs. Ron and Mary Hulnick, Co-Directors, University of Santa Monica*

"What a wonderful evening. Everyone on the path to something higher, watching a movie that was inspired by a spiritual master and his devoted student. You could feel the essence of God's call and the pure dedication of all those involved in portraying it. A must-see for anyone on a spiritual journey."
—*Dr. Ed Wagner, Chiropractor*

"*The Wayshower* combines a powerful message of hope and redemption with some expert filmaking, and the result is an uplifting movie that is food for the soul."
—*Howard Fine, Acting Coach and author of Fine on Acting*

"Thank you for making this enlightening film. As I watched the film, I saw parts of myself that I hadn't thought about in a long time. I left the theater with great insights. I laughed, loved, and learned from this movie."
—*Kristen Addix, Indigo Starlight Productions*

"We all knowingly or unknowingly live and exist on different levels or planes; call it dreaming, day dreaming, spacing out, talking to oneself,

or listening to our inner voice. *The Wayshower* brings this reality to the screen showing our quest for truth and meaning in Jesus Garcia's journey. His search for his teacher, his "Wayshower" is a universal one as we all play student and teacher simultaneously. Eric Roberts' stoic performance brings to mind Henry Fonda in *The Grapes of Wrath* while Peter Stormare is a much more unpleasant Hannibal Lecter. *The Wayshower* enlightens and demonstrates a truth we can all relate to and identify with, and fabulous actors, beautiful locations, and an emotionally touching story keep us riveted in our seats from start to finish. It did for me."
—*Laura Mola, Writer / Producer*

"I had been looking forward to seeing *The Wayshower* at Warner Bros all week even though it was my ninth time seeing it!! I find that each time I see it, it is a different experience for me. I love the cinematography and storyline, and the movie moves me deeply. I am grateful each time I am able to watch this amazing movie."
—*Dr. Kate Ferrick, Relationships Coach*

"As I prepared to attend *The Wayshower* screening, I was expecting to see the life of our beloved J-R. Instead, I found myself in a ride where no time or place could be defined just as endless as the vastness of our hearts. Jsu Garcia and crew will take you on a ride where the inner worlds will align in perfect harmony with Spirit and just not let you down."
—*Amelia Amell, Artist*

"I LOVED it. I thought the movie was incredible and cannot wait to see it again (and again). Everything about it was magical from the cinematography to the acting to the stories. Jsu, cast, and crew did an incredible job and I am so impressed and honored that I got to see it. Wow and THANK YOU to everyone involved."
—*Julie Ireland, Productivity Coach, David Allen Company*

"I watched with anticipation and was drawn to each subtle, yet profound turn of events. My teenage son sat on the edge of his seat hanging on to each exchange between the

father and his beloved teenage son, J-R, the Wayshower of our times."
—*Regina Athnos, Teacher*

"I really enjoyed *The Wayshower*. The acting and sound were superb and the film looked beautiful!"
—*Jonathan Rosenbloom, GSO Business Management*

"A touching film with a story that drew me in and kept me asking questions. I loved it."
—*Adam Carasso, Software Engineer*

"*The Wayshower* is a film with vision that anyone wondering 'who they really are' should see. It is well paced with AMAZING sound."
—*Kevin Carr, Creative Director,*
GreenTwithTamara.TV

"Viewing the movie, *The Wayshower,* was not only delightful and held my interest throughout, it also had the effect of stimulating my searching and learning new levels within myself."
—*Joe Ann Cain, Psychologist*

"*The Wayshower* presented stories John-Roger has told in his teachings, and even more, put flesh and blood on his awakening to his spiritual mission. Warmly and deeply inspiring. A great movie for all of us who are awakening to the Light."

—*John Cawley, Software Manager, Formula Consultants / Facilitator, Doctorate of Spiritual Science*

"I got an even deeper appreciation of J-R's life, of his teachings and work. I also got a clearer look at what it means to be a Spiritual Warrior by aligning my inner selves with my intentions and knowing that if I want more of Spirit, I need to step up to what's newly present."

—*Rinaldo Porcile, President, Cumbre de Lideres*